Poker Winners Are Different

Books by Dr. Alan N. Schoonmaker

Anxiety and the Executive

Executive Career Strategy

A Student's Survival Manual

Selling: The Psychological Approach

Negotiate to Win

The Psychology of Poker

Your Worst Poker Enemy (published by Lyle Stuart)

Your Best Poker Friend (published by Lyle Stuart)

Poker Winners Are Different

Get the Mental Advantage

ALAN N. SCHOONMAKER, Ph.D.

Lyle Stuart
Kensington Publishing Corp.
www.Kensingtonbooks.com

LYLE STUART BOOKS are published by

Kensington Publishing Corp.
850 Third Avenue
New York, NY 10022

All Kensington titles, imprints, and distributed lines are available at special quantity discounts for bulk purchases for sales promotions, premiums, fundraising, educational, or institutional use. Special book excerpts or customized printings can also be created to fit specific needs. For details, write or phone the office of the Kensington special sales manager: Kensington Publishing Corp., 850 Third Avenue, New York, NY 10022, attn: Special Sales Department; phone 1-800-221-2647.

Lyle Stuart and the Lyle Stuart two spade logo are Reg. US Pat. & TM Off.

First printing: March 2009

10 9 8 7 6 5 4 3 2 1

Printed in the United States of America

ISBN-13: 978-0-8184-0728-4
ISBN-10: 0-8184-0728-X

Contents

Foreword *by David Sklansky*   vii

Acknowledgments   ix

Part One: Introduction

  1. Poker Winners Are *Really* Different   3

  2. Winners Are More Motivated and Disciplined   13

  3. Winners Make Good Trade-Offs   24

  4. Winners Manage Risks and Information Very Well   42

Part Two: Winners Control Their Focus

Introduction   55

  5. Winners Focus on Long-Term Results   57

  6. Winners Focus on the Here and Now   67

  7. Winners Focus on Power   75

  8. Winners Focus on Other People   84

  9. Winners Consider Complexities   90

Part Three: Winners Control Their Thought Processes

Introduction   99

  10. Winners Are Brutally Realistic   101

  11. Winners Think Logically   111

  12. Winners Prepare Thoroughly   117

  13. Winners Concentrate Intensely   135

  14. Winners Probe Efficiently   141

  15. Winners Use Feedback Loops Well   153

Part Four: Winners Control the Information They Transmit

Introduction   169

16. Winners Are Judiciously Deceptive   174

17. Winners Create the Right Images   186

Part Five: Winners Control Their Reactions to Feelings

Introduction   199

18. Winners Accept Poker As It Is   204

19. Winners Depersonalize Conflicts   213

Part Six: Winners Act Decisively

Introduction   221

20. Winners Are Selectively Aggressive   225

21. Winners Push When They Are Winning   234

22. Winners Adjust Effectively to Changes   241

23. Winners Pay Their Dues   249

24. How to Become a Winner   257

Appendixes

A: Answers to Questions in Chapter 1   279

B: Winners' Laws   284

C: How to Break Out of Your Comfort Zone   290

Index   301

About the Author   309

Foreword

by David Sklansky

Highly successful poker players do four things:

1. Learn how to play as well as they possibly can (including making others play badly).
2. Play their best at all times.
3. Choose whichever available game offers them the greatest expected value (EV) as long as they have an adequate bankroll for it.
4. Avoid games in which they would be clearly under-bankrolled.

Duh, you might be thinking to yourself, pretty obvious. Why do things any other way if winning serious money at poker is a high priority for you? And I agree. But I also know that most aspiring poker pros do *not* always do these things, not only because they are *psychologically* difficult, but especially since they can sometimes get away *without* doing them.

Concentrating and studying are not easy things to do. Folding almost playable hands when they are your best chance to get "even" for the night takes unusual willpower. Choosing a smaller game than normal, because it offers the greatest "hourly rate" (EV–wise) in the room, means that you must give up the anticipation of making a big score that session. It also may mean that you are confronting the fact that your skill is not as great as some others who *would* expect to make more in the bigger game. The same is true if you are choosing a game smaller than you want to play because the math equations say you should not take the risk. Passing up this bigger game is even harder to do psychologically if it is particularly "juicy" or if you had previously been playing for these stakes, but presently do not have the bankroll for it.

So you see that those four techniques are not quite as easy to do as they may seem—at least for most people. There are often large psychological and emotional pressures to do something different. You have to learn how to fight those pressures.

Showing you how to fight those pressures is, of course, Dr. Alan Schoonmaker's specialty. Something he does very well in this book, along with many other things. Winners are indeed "different." But there's probably no reason you can't be one of them.

Acknowledgments

I am very lucky to have friends who help me with my books and magazine columns. They suggest topics, offer quotations, and critically review my drafts.

David Sklansky, poker's foremost theorist, has had an immense impact on my thinking. Over the past eight years, we have discussed a very wide range of topics. He also commented on much of this book's content when it was aimed at a different audience and had a different title, *Business Is a Poker Game.*

Mason Malmuth, the author and publisher of many of the best poker books, also read *Business Is a Poker Game,* and he made dozens of suggestions. Mason's and David's published works provided this book's basic organization.

Matt Lessinger (author of *The Book of Bluffs*), Barry Tanenbaum (author of *Advanced Limit Hold'em Strategy*), Dave ("Cinch") Hench (author of *The Poker World According to Cinch*), and Tommy Angelo (author of *Elements of Poker*) are very talented writers who have edited this book and many of my magazine columns. I repeatedly quote them because their ideas are so correct, original, and provocative.

Dr. Daniel Kessler, a clinical psychologist, has contributed many ideas that greatly improved the book, especially the final chapter and appendix C.

Ed Miller is the co-author of four poker books. His expertise in risk management greatly improved the chapter on that subject.

Jim Brier and I talk about poker all the time, and he has taught me a great deal. Jerry Flannigan helped me clarify my thoughts on several subjects.

I'd like to thank all the poker authors whose work I've quoted. Their published work and private conversations have taught me a great deal.

The No-limit Discussion Group and the Wednesday Poker Discussion Group have given me dozens of ideas on virtually everything related to poker.

Sharron Hoppe, my personal assistant, helped with both this book and the other tasks I neglected while writing it.

I am grateful to all of them and to the dozens of other people who have talked to me about poker and psychology.

PART ONE

Introduction

1. Poker Winners Are *Really* Different

Professional poker is a ruthless meritocracy.
　　—**Barry Tanenbaum,** professional player, coach,
　　and author[1]

Barry summarized a critical difference between poker and most other professions. You can make a living, even a good one, as a mediocre salesman, teacher, lawyer, carpenter, or doctor. Most people are mediocre, but nearly everyone makes a living. In professional poker you can't survive unless you're among the best.

In fact, *all* cardroom and online poker games are ruthless meritocracies because so few people win. Many experts estimate that— because of the rake, tips, and other expenses—85–90 percent of all cardroom and online players are long-term losers, but they have no solid data. Jay Lovinger, an ESPN columnist, says the numbers are even worse.

> There is one group that can and does track this kind of stat, though they are not about to publicize the results. That group consists of online poker site management, two members of which revealed to me . . . [that] only 8 and 7 percent, respectively, of all players on their sites finish the year in the black.[2]

---

1. Speech to the Escargot Poker Conference, February, 2003. My books contain more footnotes than other poker texts. Ignore them or use them to get more information. If you disagree with me, check the sources.

2. Jay Lovinger, "Jay Delivers the Commandments," *Page 2,* July 19, 2005, sports.espn.go.com/espn/page2/story?page=lovinger/050719&num=0

This book will help *you* become one of that small percentage of winners. If you are already winning, it will help you win more. You will see how winners and losers think, feel, and act; then learn what to do to increase your profits.

The word "loser" may offend you, but—as we just saw—most players *are* losers. Of course, there are not just winners and losers. There is a huge range from big winners to big losers, and most players are somewhere in the middle, winning or losing less.

To make it easier to see the differences between winners and losers, I will describe the extremes. However, most chapters end with a section titled How Do You Rate? There you can estimate the *degree* to which you resemble winners or losers.

Do *You* Act Like a Winner or a Loser?

Let's compare your approach to a winner's. I'll describe a few situations and give you several choices. *Pick the action you would probably take* (not the one you think is the textbook answer). Even if you don't like any alternative or like two of them, pick just one. Don't pick one that you wouldn't have considered if I hadn't mentioned it.

The "textbook answers" are in appendix A. Answer every question before looking at appendix A. Looking at any answer may affect your other answers.

Situation A

You have pocket aces in a no-limit hold'em game with $2 and $5 blinds. You push in your $100 stack. Assume that everyone has random cards. How many callers do you want?

Pick any number from one to nine.

Situation B

You're in a very soft no-limit hold'em game. An obnoxious drunk has put nearly everyone off-balance. He plays almost every hand, raises more than half the pots, and has been extremely lucky. He has a huge stack. Despite playing your usual solid game, you're losing heavily. He's given you three terrible beats and needled you every time. He even said, "You don't have the guts to play good poker." Then he laughed at you. What would you do?

- Ignore him, keep playing a solid game, but adjust to his wild play and its effects on the other players.
- Say, "You're an idiot, and you're going to lose that stack."
- Explain why you play such a solid game.
- Change tables.
- Go home.
- Loosen up to show everyone that you're not afraid of him.
- _____

Situation C

You were a steady winner at $20–$40 limit hold'em, but you're on a terrible losing streak. You lost $6,000 in the past two months, and financial pressures forced you to take $4,000 from your poker bankroll to fix your roof. Your bankroll is down to $2,000. You see seats open in four games. Which game will you join?

- A tight-passive $10–$20 game. Nearly everyone is weak-tight, and nobody is at all aggressive or tricky. You can beat them because they are easy to read and bluff. Of course, you cannot beat them for much.
- A fairly typical $20–$40 game. You are better than all but two players, and those two are about your equal.
- A wild $15–$30 game with huge pots. There are two ma-

niacs, three loose-passive players, two strangers, and two moderately competent players.

- A loose-passive $15–$30 game. Six players are loose-passive, two are moderately competent, and one is a stranger.

Situation D

Tomorrow you will play at your first final table of a high buy-in, no-limit hold'em tournament. You will have an average stack. Five of tomorrow's opponents are highly regarded pros. You have played against only two of them, but your friends have played against all of them. You know the other four players, and they are about as good as you are.

Even if you finish tenth, it'll be your biggest payday. If you finish first, it'll change your life. You're so nervous that you're afraid you won't sleep well tonight or play well tomorrow.

It's 9 P.M., and the final table will start at noon tomorrow. Assume that you can take only one of these actions. What will you do between now and then?

- Ask your friends for suggestions about how to play against the pros, especially the ones you have never faced. But make sure that you get to bed by 2 A.M.
- Study *Harrington on Hold'em, Volume II: The Endgame.* You bought it, but never read it. Now might be a good time to study it because it focuses on the endgame.
- Go to bed immediately. Since you know that you won't sleep without help, take sleeping pills. Unfortunately, they often give you a "hangover."
- Take two glasses of wine just before playing to steady your nerves.

Situation E

You're playing in your usual $1–$2 blinds no-limit game. You bought in for the maximum of $200 and lost it almost immediately when your aces got cracked by kings. You lost your second $200 buy-in when you raised with ace-king, flopped a king, bet aggressively on the flop, went all-in on the turn, and lost to a flopped set of nines. Your third buy-in and half of your fourth one were lost more slowly.

You can't seem to do anything right. If you have a hand, you don't get action or you get beaten. When you bluff, you get called, sometimes by players with weak hands. You have never lost $700 in one night, and it's really bothering you.

You have $500 in your pocket and another $1,000 in your checking account. You can withdraw up to $1,000 with your ATM card, but must leave $800 in your account to pay your rent. What will you do?

- Go home immediately.
- Keep playing, but promise yourself that you will quit if you lose your $100 stack.
- Rebuy immediately and, if necessary, keep rebuying until your cash runs out and then quit. Promise yourself that you will quit then.
- Keep rebuying and, if necessary, use your ATM card to take out the $200 you don't need for your rent. But promise yourself that you won't touch the rent money.
- Switch to the $2–$5 no-limit game. You know only two players, but the game looks pretty soft.

Situation F

You're playing with your closest friend and notice that he has a completely reliable tell that he is bluffing. What would you do?

- Tell him immediately and quietly what it is.
- Wait for a good time; then pull him aside and tell him what it is.
- Keep quiet and use it against him.

Compare all your answers to appendix A, and then come back here.

What Have You Learned About Yourself?

Compare your answers to the textbook answers, then *write* what you learned about yourself in the blank space below. You may not want to do it, but analyzing yourself is an essential self-development step.

Later chapters will help you to compare yourself to winners and losers on many dimensions. It won't be fun, and you may even get annoyed at me. But—if you want to become one of the handful of winners—you have to do many unpleasant things.

The biggest difference between winners and losers is that losers do what makes them comfortable, but winners do whatever gets the best long-term results.

Why Should You Read This Book?

Are you satisfied with your results? If you are, don't read this book. If not, read on. You've tried to improve your game by reading books, watching videos, and talking to friends. Perhaps you're winning a little more or losing a little less than before, but you still aren't satisfied. Why hasn't your increased knowledge and skill produced better results?

The answer is simple: you're not thinking, feeling, or acting like a winner. Winners have a fundamentally different approach to poker, and you probably can't win big without copying it. *The critical first step toward becoming a winner is to change the way you think about poker and yourself.*

Winners Are *Not* Necessarily More Skillful or Talented

If you asked, "How are winners different from losers?" most people would answer, "They play better." That answer is true, of course, but it misses the point. Greater skill is *not* the most important difference.

It certainly helps, but many strong players fail, while weaker ones succeed. You may know excellent players who are often broke and moderately skilled ones who win consistently and always have money. In fact, some *world-class* players are broke. Despite their immense skills, they are losers.

I am *not* kidding. Johnny Moss and Stu Ungar are generally regarded as the best players of their eras, and both died broke. So did

Hall of Famer, Nick "The Greek" Dandolos. The same may happen to some of today's top pros.

Nolan Dalla, the media director for The World Series of Poker, has been reporting on tournaments for many years. He wrote, "One of the most troubling aspects of the tournament circuit is seeing how many players are constantly broke. I'm not talking about bad poker players or novices. I'm talking about names and faces everyone would recognize."[3]

They are broke because of poor emotional control, an inability to evaluate themselves objectively, a need to challenge tougher players, and many other reasons. An important, but rarely discussed reason is that they are not much better than their opponents. "Your success at poker depends, not on how well you play, but on how well you play in relation to your opponents."[4] If most players in a game have approximately equal abilities, the small differences in abilities will have little effect. It is an extremely well-verified statistical principle. For example, research proves that Scholastic Aptitude Tests (SAT) scores are poor predictors of grades in elite colleges because they accept only the highest scorers.

I am writing this book during the Olympics, and the same principle is extremely obvious there. The Olympians are such superb athletes that the differences between them are tiny. The winner in an event may be a few hundredths of a second faster than the second, third, and fourth place finishers, while any of them would finish far ahead of nearly every non-Olympian.

The same principle applies to poker because most games are "stratified." As games get bigger, the players get tougher. The skill differences between high-, middle-, and low-stakes players are often

3. Nolan Dalla, "So You Wanna Be a Tournament Pro? Fuhgetaboutit!" *Poker Pages,* www.pokerpages.com/articles/archives/dalla27.htm.

4. Cooke, Roy, "A Great Game?" *Card Player,* May 10, 2002, 14.

much greater than the differences between players in most games at any level. "We cannot stress enough that—in the bigger games—most of the worst players are good enough to beat the smaller games."[5]

If poker players and Olympians compete only against weaker opposition, they will nearly always win. In addition, it doesn't matter whether you win an Olympic event by a hundredth of a second or ten minutes. You still get the gold medal. In poker you want to win as much as possible, and the easiest way to win a lot of bets is to play against much weaker players.

The subjects this book discusses have much greater effects on your results than your knowledge or skill because the differences between players are *huge.* In most games the skill differences between players are *much* smaller than the differences in their motives, discipline, thoughts, reactions to feelings, and decisiveness. These differences are the core of this book.

That's good news because you're stuck with your natural ability. It came from your genes and history, and you can't change them. However, with hard work you can change some of these characteristics. This book can help you to become a winner, *regardless of how talented you are.*

Winners' Laws

That's enough discussion. You want to know what you should *do.* Most chapters contain this short section that shifts the emphasis from analysis to action.

---

5. Ray Zee and David Fromm, with Alan Schoonmaker, *World Class High Stakes and Short-Handed Limit Hold'em.* Not yet published.

1. Learn how you compare to winners.

That's this book's first objective. It describes how winners think, feel, and act to help you compare yourself to them. You may dislike some comparisons, but you should learn what they are.

2. Commit yourself to making the necessary changes.

Learning these comparisons is just the first step. If you don't commit yourself to changing toward the winners' patterns, this book will waste your time and money. If you can't or won't make that commitment, you'll continue to get the same, disappointing results. It really is that brutally simple.

2. Winners Are More Motivated and Disciplined

> *To win at poker, one must want to win. More importantly, one's subconscious mind must want to win! ... The poker player who can't control his mental and emotional state will never be a winner, and it doesn't matter how much experience, natural talent, money, or knowledge he possesses.*
>
> —Jason Misa[1]

Winners have *both* an intense desire to win and extreme self-control. Like the "rational man" of classical economic theory, they do whatever it takes to maximize their long-term profits.

They work harder, study longer, remain more alert, act more deceptively, avoid games they can't beat, attack more ruthlessly, criticize themselves more harshly, refuse to yield to their emotions, and *always insist on having an edge.* They make these and many other sacrifices that most people won't make. In fact, they are so competitive that they may feel that they're not sacrificing anything important. Everything but winning is hardly worth thinking about.

You may think that it is unhealthy to compete so compulsively. I agree and have argued forcefully that—from a mental health perspective—you should be more balanced.[2]

But this book concerns *only* winning, and everything you feel, think, or do that conflicts with that goal will reduce your profits.

---

1. Jason Misa "The Ultimate Poker Skill," *Card Player,* November 28, 1998, 73.

2. Alan Schoonmaker, "Don't Take Poker Too Seriously," in *Your Worst Poker Enemy* (NY: Lyle Stuart, 2007), 305–315.

You must decide how important winning is to you and how high a price you will pay for it. Some people naively assume that they can win without making sacrifices. They will certainly be disappointed.

What's the bottom line? *Unless you have* both *an intense desire and extreme self-control, you probably won't do all it takes to become a big winner.*

An Intense, Ruthless Need to Win

That drive is the starting point. Without it you won't be willing to make all those sacrifices. The best poker players are like Larry Bird, a member of basketball's Hall of Fame. Red Auerbach, his coach, once said, "Larry doesn't come to play. He comes to *win.*"

Poker winner's competitiveness is almost unrelated to what the money will buy. They need to win, not so that they can buy more toys, but because they define themselves by how much they win.

They are also more ruthless than intense competitors in most games because poker is a negative-sum game. Business, the stock market, real estate, and many other "games," are partly win-win, but poker is purely win-lose. Your profits always come at someone else's expense.

Poker is much tougher than most win-lose games because they are zero-sum, but—because of the house's charges—the winners' profits are always less than the loser's losses. Unless you ruthlessly seek and exploit edges, those charges will eat you up.

Poker is also a predatory game. All successful predators follow a simple rule: attack the weakest, most vulnerable prey. You make most of your money, not by outsmarting the better players, but by exploiting the weaker ones. It's the exact opposite of the values you have been taught: Be honest. Fight fair. Pick on somebody your own size. Be gentle toward the weak.

His ruthlessness helped Jack Straus to become a Poker Hall of

Famer. He once said, "I'd bust my own grandmother if she played poker with me." Countless poker players agree, and their ruthlessness gives them a *huge* edge. *"If you are not driven to win and play against equally talented, but much more ruthless competitors, you are going to lose."*[3]

Losers lack the winners' single-mindedness. They want to satisfy many needs, but these needs conflict with each other. Focusing solely on profits may not feel right, and it's not as much fun. They want to challenge tough games and players; they feel guilty about being deceitful; they ache to criticize fools who make terrible mistakes and give them bad beats; and they don't want to beat up weak relatives and friends. They try to satisfy all their motives by doing a bit of this and a little of that, which prevents them from winning as much as more single-minded competitors.

Some winners don't believe that their attitude is abnormal. They feel contempt for people who don't put winning above everything, and they certainly can't understand them. For "normal" people (aka "losers") poker is just a game. They play it for many reasons, but primarily for pleasure. Of course, they like to win, but they can enjoy poker even when they lose. In many games some losers are having a good time and some winners are miserable (because they aren't winning enough to satisfy their insatiable needs).

Insatiable needs are a sign of psychological problems and a source of constant dissatisfaction, but all I'm discussing now is profitability. If you want to maximize it, you have to put the bottom line ahead of *everything*.

---

3. Alan Schoonmaker, "Would You Bust Your Own Grandmother?" pages 105–115 of *Your Best Poker Friend* (NY: Lyle Stuart, 2007) discussed the effects of ruthlessness.

Extreme Discipline

This quality is as important as the drive to win. Without that drive you won't be *willing* to make the sacrifices, but without extreme self-control, you won't be *able* to make them. Winners are extremely disciplined.

Barry Greenstein, a great player, certainly agrees. His book, *Ace on the River,* contains a list of the twenty-five traits of winning players. "In control of their emotions" was fourth, and his list included several other self-control qualities:

- Persistent was sixteenth.
- Able to think under pressure was eighth.
- Honest with themselves was second.
- Psychologically tough was first. The best don't give in, no matter how severe the psychological beating."[4]

Winners' discipline affects every element of their game. They fold hands they want to play. They resist their desires to challenge tough players. They push aside their pity for vulnerable players and mercilessly attack them. They force themselves to concentrate. They resist the impulse to criticize bad players. They objectively assess their own play and get feedback from coaches and friends. *They have the discipline to do the unpleasant things that losers won't do.*

4. Barry Greenstein, *Ace on the River* (Fort Collins, CO: Last Knight, 2005).

The Need for Balance

Without enough self-control, an obsessive need to win can destroy you. You would be like an extremely powerful racing car with a broken steering system. I call these uncontrolled people "supercompetitors." They have two major weaknesses:

1. They can't accept their own limitations.
2. They always need to win, even when the issues are trivial.

Both problems are caused by denying reality about themselves and poker. Winners accept their limitations and recognize that they can't always win. They make intelligent trade-offs, sacrificing some satisfactions and accepting unimportant defeats to do the only thing that really matters, *getting the chips.*

Supercompetitors look macho, but they are really so insecure that they have to prove something. They pay a high price for their insecurity. Some very talented supercompetitors severely harm themselves by:

1. Playing above their bankrolls.
2. Choosing games that are too tough for them.
3. Challenging the toughest players in those games.
4. Overreacting to bad beats and other losses.
5. Continuing to play, trying desperately to get even, because they can't accept a losing session.
6. Criticizing weak players and arguing about trivial issues.

Supercompetitors generally deny the truth about themselves. Instead of admitting that they are insecure, they rationalize that they take many of these actions (especially numbers 1–3) to gain the experience they need to develop themselves. They also would

not admit that showing off their "superiority" by winning arguments is more important to them than increasing their profits.

The opposite extreme is also destructive: *if your self-control out-
weighs your motivation, you won't act decisively.* Hamlet was a classic case: His famous "To be or not to be" soliloquy summarized his
entire life. He could not make up his mind about anything, not
even killing himself.

Indecisive poker players haven't got a chance, but you may
know some of them, including a few who understand poker theory.
They try to avoid commitments by checking when they should bet
and folding or calling when they should raise.

Winners balance their intense drive to win and self-control. If
the stakes are too low or they have won so much that they feel complacent or they have other things on their mind, they won't care
enough to play well. Conversely, if the stakes are too high or they
are losing heavily or they are risking the rent money, they will lack
the essential detachment and control. Winners constantly monitor
themselves, and if they are not *both* motivated and controlled, they
take a break or go home.

Winners' Laws

As in the last and most future chapters, the Winners' Laws shift
from analysis to action. They tell you what *you* should do to apply
a chapter's principles.

1. Accept a painful reality: intense, ruthless competitors have a HUGE edge.

You may wish that normal, balanced people were not at such a
disadvantage, but you *must* accept that reality. If you compete
against people who are equally talented, but much hungrier, you
will lose.

2. Accept another painful reality: you can't make huge changes in your competitive drives and talent.

They are like your poker cards. Since you can't change them, you must accept them and use them well. Many self-help books about other subjects exhort you to be totally committed to success, to ignore your limitations, "to reach for the stars," "to dream the impossible dream," and so on, but such exhortations are silly.

- You want what you want, not what other people say you *should* want.
- Your talent is like your height; you may want to be taller, but it won't happen.

So accept yourself as you are, and don't feel guilty about not being what you can never be.

3. Assess your own talent and motivation honestly.

Since you can't change them, you must know what they are. The next chapter contains procedures for assessing your motives. Now we will focus primarily on one question: How talented are you?

Without answering that question, you can't make intelligent plans. For example, unless you have immense talent and commitment, you have *no* chance to become a world-class player. That fact is obvious, yet many merely competent and a few mediocre players have told me they can become stars.

After looking at yourself, apply the same logic you use with your cards. It is not how good they are, but *how they compare to those of the other players.* A flush is a good hand, unless someone has a better one. You may be more talented, motivated, and controlled than most people, but your competition is not average people.

The average IQ is exactly 100, but that average includes everyone from idiots to geniuses. Retarded people rarely play poker, but many extremely intelligent people do. I'd estimate that the average cardroom player's IQ is about 115, and the average is higher in larger games. The same pattern exists for most other qualities such as motivation, discipline, theoretical knowledge, and skills: the bigger the game, the tougher the competition. The critical question is not how intelligent, motivated, disciplined, and so on you are; it is *How do you compare to the people in your game and in every game you want to play?*

Motivation is essential, but it cannot overcome a huge difference in talent. If I played tennis with a top player, I would be extremely motivated, and he would be bored. But I would not have a chance. The opposite principle applies if talent is nearly equal. If two tennis pros have slightly different talents, but the less talented one is more committed, he will probably be more successful. He will practice harder, analyze his game more critically, keep in better shape, and do other things that his more talented, but less motivated competitor, may neglect.

Unfortunately, the same factors that cause losers to overestimate themselves cause them to underestimate the competition. They think that their competitors aren't really more talented and committed. They are just lucky or whatever other excuse the losers can invent. To succeed you must *objectively* compare yourself to your competition.

4. Work on your self-control.

You can increase it, but it won't be easy. Of course, no poker authority ever says that winning is easy. Understanding and accepting your limitations are critical steps toward increasing your self-control. Then you must constantly monitor your actions and motives.

When you are making important decisions, ask yourself: *Why am I making this decision?* If you have thoroughly analyzed the situation and sincerely believe that your decision will increase your profits, it will probably do so. If you have not thoroughly analyzed the situation or if you are driven by other motives, you will probably reduce your profits.

How Do You Rate?

Most chapters end with this question, and it may be the most important one. You may dislike self-analysis, but deliberately comparing yourself to winners will help you plan your development. You will get the most benefit if you take four steps for every rating scale:

1. Rate yourself as objectively as possible.
2. Ask one or more people who know you well to rate you.
3. Compare your ratings and discuss any differences. Why did your ratings agree or disagree?
4. Discuss the ratings' implications. What should you do about them?

You will compare yourself to winners by indicating how much you agree or disagree with various statements. These statements often contain extreme words such as "always," "completely," and "never." Of course, hardly anyone is extreme enough to be rated a 7 or a 1. In fact, if you have several extremely high or low ratings, you are probably not being objective. Rating your agreement or disagreement with extreme statements is a standard psychometric technique.

There are two rating scales, one for motivation and one for self-control.

Your Motivation

Rate **only** *your desire to maximize your profits.* You may also be extremely competitive about sports, sex, winning arguments, or being the center of attention. These drives suggest that you're a supercompetitor, and they are usually liabilities. They divert your attention and cause other people to react negatively to you. Winners focus their extreme competitiveness on winning the chips. If other competitive drives are so important that they cost you chips, *reduce* your rating.

Circle the number that best describes how much you agree with this statement: *While playing poker, I am intensely competitive. I will do almost anything to maximize my profits.* (7) Agree strongly, (6) Agree, (5) Agree somewhat, (4) Neutral, (3) Disagree somewhat, (2) Disagree, (1) Disagree strongly.

Circle that number in the appropriate place in "The How Do You Rate? Data" section on page 258.

Your Discipline

Circle the number that best describes your agreement with this statement: *While playing poker, I am extremely disciplined. I can control myself no matter what happens.* (7) Agree strongly, (6) Agree, (5) Agree somewhat, (4) Neutral, (3) Disagree somewhat, (2) Disagree, (1) Disagree strongly.

Circle that number in the appropriate place on page 259.

When you finish the book, that chapter will contain all your self-ratings to help you see the overall picture. It then recommends ways to become the winner you want to be.

The Critical Questions

Review this chapter, especially the Winners' Laws and How Do You Rate? sections. Then answer two questions:

1. What are the implications of both my self-ratings?
2. What should I do differently? List the *specific actions* you should take to increase your self-control.

Discuss your answers with someone you trust and take good notes.

3. Winners Make Good Trade-Offs

There is no such thing as a free lunch.
—**Milton Friedman,** Nobel Laureate in Economics

Professor Friedman certainly wasn't the first person to say that, but he frequently repeated it. He knew that many people believed that they could have free lunches, such as more government benefits with lower taxes. They couldn't accept that somebody must pay for everything.

As far as I know, he never played or wrote about poker. He concentrated on the disastrous effects that believing in free lunches had on political, social, and economic policies. But the same belief devastates many poker players. They try to get everything—profits, fun, relaxation, challenges, status, fame, and so on—because they deny the reality that winning poker demands painful trade-offs.

The actions that satisfy some motives will frustrate others. If you don't understand, accept, and work within the limitations created by this reality, you'll make some very bad decisions. Good trade-offs sacrifice lower priority motives to satisfy higher priority ones. To make them you must:

- Know what you want.
- Analyze the costs and benefits of each alternative.
- Select the alternative that offers the best cost/benefit ratio.

Why Do You Play Poker?

Your long-term success depends on complex trade-offs that involve at least four factors:

1. Your motives
2. Your talent
3. Your readiness to work hard
4. Your ruthlessness

Start by analyzing your motives because they affect almost everything, including your readiness to work hard and your ruthlessness. Many losers don't analyze their own motives, nor do they think in terms of trading one satisfaction for another.

Some motives hardly affect or even reinforce each other. For example, wanting to play this hand very well increases both your short- and long-term profits. The desire to develop yourself is closely related to the desire to challenge tough players.

Many poker authors assume that players have only one motive—to win the most money, but it's a ridiculous assumption. Since most players lose, there must be other motives; otherwise, the losers wouldn't play. And everyone—even the most profit-hungry professional—takes many profit-reducing actions.

Even if they don't assume that your only motive is to make money, many authorities insist that it's the only one you *should* have. But their insistence ignores a psychological reality: you want what you want, not what other people say you *should* want.

Don't kid yourself about why you play poker. Instead, try to assess the importance of various motives by completing a little questionnaire.[1]

The procedure is quite simple: Just divide your total motivation (100%) into as many pieces as you think are correct. For example, if your only motive is to make money and you treat poker as just a job, assign 100 percentage points to "Make money."

1. The next few paragraphs and the questionnaire were taken from pages 34–36 of Alan Schoonmaker's *The Psychology of Poker* (Henderson, NV: Two Plus Two, 2000). Since I made some changes, I omitted quotation marks.

If your primary motive is to make money, but you also enjoy socializing and meeting people, like to test yourself against competitive challenges, get a little kick from gambling, and want to pass
time, you may rate Make money 40%, Socialize 20%, Competitive
challenge 20%, Excitement of gambling 10%, and Pass time 10%.

If you really don't care about making money, if the chips are just
scorekeeping tokens, you may assign all your points to other cate-
gories.

If you have motives other than the ones listed, write them in the
blank spaces and assign numbers to them.

Use a pencil or a computer so that you can make changes, and
make sure that your numbers add exactly to 100%.[2] After completing the following questionnaire, copy your answers in the identical
questionnaire on pages 259–60.

Why Do You Play Poker?
Make money   _____ %

Socialize, meet people   _____ %

Relax   _____ %

Get excitement of gambling   _____ %

Test yourself against tough competition   _____ %

Develop your skills   _____ %

Get sense of accomplishment from winning   _____ %

---

2. Dividing percentages this way oversimplifies the situation because some motives reinforce or don't affect each other.

Get status and fame   _____%

Pass time   _____%

Other (specify)

_____   _____%

_____   _____%

_____   _____%

Total (must be 100%)   _____%

Note that this procedure automatically forces you to make trade-offs. To increase the points for one motive, you must reduce the points assigned to others. Note also that the higher your score for "make money," the more likely you are to sacrifice other motives. The opposite is also true. The more important other drives are to you, the more frequently you will take profit-reducing actions. From a purely economic point of view, it pays to want nothing from poker but profits.

Specific Trade-Offs

Now that we have an overall picture of your motives, let's look at some specific trade-offs. Each one is followed by a seven-point rating scale. Rate yourself by circling a number. Then circle the same number in the How Do You Rate? Data section starting on page 260.

Profits vs. Fun

It's the most basic trade-off, and many losers won't make it. They want to have fun, but still win. They just can't accept that they have to sacrifice fun to increase profits. So they play too many hands, chase too long, and make other enjoyable, but costly mistakes.

I once wrote: "One of the most fascinating poker questions is: Why do so many people play so badly? ... The answer is surprisingly simple: *it's more fun to play badly than well.* Of course, winning is more fun than losing, but trying to maximize our profits would force us to do lots of unpleasant things. In fact, profit-maximization makes such extreme demands that only a few extraordinarily disciplined people play their best game most of the time, and *nobody* always plays it."[3]

The biggest reason that many people lose is that they do what they enjoy, not what it takes to win. Sacrificing fun is part of the price of success, and you won't win without paying it.

Indicate where you stand on this trade-off by circling the appropriate number:

Profits						Fun
7	6	5	4	3	2	1

Profits vs. Avoiding Frustrations

Many decisions will increase both your profits and your frustrations. For example, if you increase your profits by playing against certain kinds of weak players, they will frustrate you by giving you bad beats, talking too much, not knowing what the action is, delaying the game while they order drinks, and so on.

---

3. Alan Schoonmaker, "Fun vs. Profit," *Card Player,* June 20, 2003.

Indicate where you stand on this trade-off by circling the appropriate number:

Profits   Lower Frustration

7   6   5   4   3   2   1

Rewards vs. Risks

Economists have discussed this trade-off for centuries. To increase profits, you must normally take greater risks. Poker winners understand and apply that principle, even if they have never read an economics book.

The critical issue is whether the probability and personal value of greater profits compensates for the higher risks. Sometimes the risks outweigh the chances for larger profits, at least for some players. For example, they may believe that the chance to make more money in higher-stakes games does not justify the higher risks. Many good players are tempted to move up, but others play at a level they can beat consistently. They deliberately trade the chances for higher profits to get smaller, but safer ones.

One reason for caution is that many players are undercapitalized. They don't have remotely as much as the authorities recommend. The win rate decreases (in big bets per hour [BBPH]) and the standard deviation (in BBPH) increases as games get larger because the competition gets tougher. Bigger games therefore create larger swings and a greater risk of going broke for undercapitalized players.

Winners trade the opportunity for larger immediate profits for increased chances to survive. They play at safe limits, build their bankrolls, and move upward slowly. Losers—including some excellent players—refuse to make that trade-off, move up too quickly, and go broke.

Playing above their bankroll hurts them in two ways: they do not have the capital to survive the inevitable losses, and they play poorly because they cannot afford to take necessary risks. It is called "playing with scared money."

Indicate where you stand on this trade-off by circling the appropriate number. This scale is a bit different from the preceding one. Everybody loves profits, but you may dislike risks. If you will take large risks to get large profits, circle a higher number:

Risks					Profits	
7	6	5	4	3	2	1

Profits vs. Variance

This trade-off appears similar to the last one, but it is quite different. It is also closely related to frustration tolerance. Some people play too passively because it *seems* less risky than playing aggressively. They check when they should bet, or they call when they should raise, even though the aggressive actions could be more profitable and *less* risky. Passive play often saves a bet, but loses a pot.

Many situations and strategies increase *both* your profits and your variance, but some people won't take them. For example, extremely tight-passive Rocks fold many positive EV (+EV) hands, don't raise with good draws and many opponents, and sacrifice profits in other ways to reduce their variance.

Countless people avoid very loose games because they're too frustrated by variance, especially bad beats. You can't get a bad beat without having the best of it, often by five or ten to one. Whining that "these people call with anything" is obviously foolish. You should *want* them to call with weak hands, even though you will occasionally lose.

But the winners' objective is long-term profits. If you really want to maximize them, you will often have to join games and make plays that increase both your variance and your frustration. You must decide whether the increased profits are more important to you than the variance and frustration.

That decision may depend on other factors. For example, if your bankroll is small or a losing streak has reduced your confidence, you may be unable to afford—financially or psychologically—a high-variance game. You may need to win more frequently, even if your wins are smaller. Your rating today could be quite different from what it would be when your bankroll or state of mind is improved.

Indicate where you stand on this trade-off by circling the appropriate number:

Profits					Variance	
7	6	5	4	3	2	1

Profits vs. Fame and Status

The desire for status and fame wasn't one of the motives in *The Psychology of Poker*. When I wrote it, hardly any poker players were famous. Now, with poker on television so frequently, some players are celebrities, and thousands more are wannabes.

Of course, poker has always had a status hierarchy. Winners are higher status than losers. Players in larger games have higher status, even if they don't do as well. A breakeven $30–$60 player has higher status than a winning $4–$8 player. Nobody really knows how much anyone wins, and many people lie about their results.

Until a few years ago, many pros did not want other people to know how good they were. A tough reputation would reduce their profits. Some people would not join their games, and others would not give them much action.

When televised tournaments became popular, some top cash

game players who had avoided tournaments started playing in them. A few said they did it because people asked, "If you're so good, why haven't I seen you on television?"

Being on television is a very mixed blessing. Players don't get much or any of the television revenue. The exposure does increase a few top pros' incomes from endorsements, and so on. However, being on television probably reduces their playing profits. Their opponents record and study their play and then use that knowledge against them *indefinitely.*

So why do they do it? Because it's a huge kick to be on television, and many pros will sacrifice substantial profits to get there. In addition, since they can't tell how much it affects their playing profits, they may rationalize that they aren't losing much (or anything).

Preston Oade, a good tournament player with whom I collaborate occasionally, e-mailed me about the conflicting desires for profits, fame, and status:

> If profits are the *only* way we keep score in poker, why does everyone seem to care about WSOP bracelets? And why have a "Player of the Year" competition based on one's overall results in designated tournaments? I suggest that the practical realities of tournament play are largely inconsistent with profit as the driving motive or as the "only" way to keep score. It is *much* easier to win money in cash games.

Indicate where you stand on this trade-off by circling the appropriate number:

Profits   Fame and Status

7   6   5   4   3   2   1

Profits vs. Testing Yourself Against Tough Competition

The desire to challenge tougher players has destroyed countless bankrolls. Even though they know that it's risky, some people can't resist the challenge. You may know players who moved too high and went bust, and you may have done it yourself. It's a natural human desire. You want to know how good you are. But yielding to that desire can be extremely expensive.

Barry Greenstein told our discussion group that he and the other regulars in Bobby's Room at the Bellagio love to have the winners of big tournaments join their games. They are so puffed up from winning a huge prize and being televised that they want to challenge Barry Greenstein, Doyle Brunson, Dan Negreanu, Jennifer Harman, and the other great players. They usually lose heavily, sometimes hundreds of thousands of dollars.

You aren't a tournament hotshot, but—if you have an excessive need to test yourself—you could be headed for very big trouble.

Indicate where you stand on this trade-off by circling the appropriate number:

Profit					Testing Yourself	
7	6	5	4	3	2	1

Profits vs. Developing Your Skills

This desire relates to every game, even ones you don't play for money. It also interacts with drives such as the one to test yourself, and we must distinguish between immediate and long-term profits.

To maximize your immediate profits, play in the softest possible games. But—if you don't sacrifice some immediate profits—you won't develop the skills you need to beat larger games. Matt Lessinger's forcefully stated his readiness to make this trade-off:

There are times (and it may surprise you that I am saying this) that I play and do not expect to make a profit. I have played in games in which my EV was very clearly negative. . . . [They] were learning experiences, and thus well worth the sacrifice. I was willing to pay my "tuition" in order to get schooled.[4]

Unfortunately, you may rationalize that you're trying to develop your skills when your primary motives are the needs to gamble and to challenge tougher players.

Indicate where you stand on this trade-off by circling the appropriate number:

Quick Profit   Developing Your Skills

7   6   5   4   3   2   1

Profits vs. Affection

We all want to be liked, but some players dislike winners, even if they are pleasant people. They take other people's money, hurting both their wallets and their egos. Winners accept being disliked as part of the price of success, but some losers deliberately trade money for affection. For example, they don't bet when they have the nuts, or they show a winning hand without their bet being called. These actions may make them more popular, but they obviously reduce their profits.

Indicate where you stand on this trade-off by circling the appropriate number:

Profit   Affection

7   6   5   4   3   2   1

4. Matt Lessinger, "Less Is Back for More," *Card Player,* June 6, 2003.

Profits vs. Being Deceptive and Exploitative

This trade-off is closely related to the previous one, and it makes some people extremely uncomfortable. Winners constantly deceive opponents, and they exploit every advantage. Many winners will do whatever the rules allow, while many losers are restrained by their scruples or fear of being disliked. For example, they may be so uncomfortable that they don't bluff often enough, or they may refuse to take advantage of a beginner, drunk, or tilted player. They'll certainly win less than equally skilled, but more deceptive or ruthless players.

Indicate where you stand on this trade-off by circling the appropriate number:

					Being Deceptive	
Profit					and Exploitative	
7	6	5	4	3	2	1

Profits vs. Ego Building

Winners forego ego building to increase their profits. They don't try to prove anything, assess their strengths and weakness honestly, select soft games, attack the weakest players, and avoid the toughest ones.

Many losers do exactly the opposite. They sacrifice profits to build their egos. They may take reckless chances to prove they are macho gamblers, criticize weak players, challenge tough ones, and brag about their brilliant plays. These actions may make them feel good, but cost them lots of money.

They also refuse to assess their abilities honestly. They don't want to know why they lose. Instead, they just complain about bad luck to protect their egos. If you doubt me, just ask yourself one question: "Why do you hear so many bad beat stories?" People tell

them all the time—even though they give away valuable information—to protect their egos by blaming losses on bad luck.

Indicate where you stand on this trade-off by circling the appropriate number:

Profit   Ego Building
7   6   5   4   3   2   1

Winners' Laws

This chapter has six Winners' Laws, and the first one is the most
important and unpleasant.

1. Accept that trade-offs are unavoidable.

Professor Friedman won the Nobel Prize because he understood
and accepted reality. He preached that we must realistically analyze
both costs and benefits because we can't avoid trade-offs. He in-
sisted that refusing to make trade-offs and demanding everything
is disastrous.

2. Accept that you can't satisfy all your motives.

You must also accept this corollary, *you must sacrifice some desires to satisfy others.* If you don't plan your trade-offs, they'll be
made for you, and they probably won't fit your priorities.

3. Understand your own motives and priorities.

Since you have to pay for everything you get, you must understand the importance of various motives and the amount you will
pay to satisfy each one.

4. Learn which trade-offs each game or strategy requires.

Since each game or strategy requires somewhat different trade-offs, you have to learn what they are and then relate them to your own priorities. You can win more money in a higher-stakes game, but the risks are *much* greater. You can make larger immediate profits by playing against only weak players, but you'll be frustrated by bad beats and you won't develop the skills you need to move up and increase your long-term profits.

If you play very tightly, you will have low variance, but win less money. If you become more aggressive in tournaments, you will cash less often, but have a better chance to take first place.

5. Don't kid yourself.

Because various motives are not clearly defined and they conflict and overlap with each other, you can easily rationalize. Instead of admitting your real reasons for doing certain things, you may give good, but false, reasons.

For example, you may play above your skill level and bankroll to get the kicks of taking foolish risks and challenging tougher players, but not admit it. Instead, you may claim that you're doing it to develop your skills so that you can increase your long-term profits. You may even be partially right. Most actions are taken for many motives, not just one. So take a hard look at your decisions and ask yourself, *Why* did I do that?

6. Make the trade-offs that fit your priorities.

Pick the situations and strategies that are most likely to satisfy your most important motives. These motives are closely related to your personal definition of "winning," which I will discuss momentarily.

For example, if you're a multimillionaire, want status and fame, and don't really care about your profits, the tournament trail may be ideal. Conversely, if you're supporting a family and want a normal family life, don't even think about the tournament circuit.

Or let's say that you have an adequate but not huge bankroll and have a strong need to maximize your current income. However, you also want to develop your game so that you can move up and make more money. If you choose larger, tougher games, the risks may be too high. If you play only in weak games, you won't develop the skills you need to move up someday. You can balance these motives by:

- Selecting games with a mixture of weak and tough players.
- Avoiding the tough players most of the time.
- Studying the tough players.
- Challenging them only when the cards and position favor you.

This sort of complicated compromise can be made only when you thoroughly understand your own motives and objectively appraise both your own and your opponents' abilities. If you aren't objective, you'll almost certainly make bad trade-offs.

How Do You Rate?

This chapter has asked many questions in unusual ways. You have rated your motives by assigning percentages to them and circling numbers. It's time to see what all this information means.

Look at the overall pattern, especially inconsistencies between the distribution of percentage points, your trade-off ratings, and—most importantly—your actions when you play poker. For example, you may have assigned a higher percentage to "make money" than to "fame and status" but frequently pass up juicy cash games to play in tough tournaments.

If you see an inconsistency, something is wrong. A certain motive seems to be more or less important than you originally thought. So re-assess your motives.

Your Personal Definition of "Winning"

Your belief about whether you are a winner or loser depends ultimately upon your definition of winning. If you do not clearly understand that definition, you will probably do things that take you in the wrong direction. For example, if you really want to become a top player, you *must* challenge tough players and tough games even if you drastically reduce your immediate income. Conversely, if you care only about grinding out the maximum immediate income, you should *never* challenge tough players and games.

Write your answers to the critical questions:

- What is my personal definition of winning?

- What are the implications of that answer?

You may see that your definition of winning is very different from the standard one, "maximizing your long-term profits." The closer your definition is to the standard one, the more willing you will be to sacrifice fun, and so on to increase your profits.

Conversely, if you have a nonstandard definition, you won't make some sacrifices. For example, you may be unwilling to increase your profits in certain ways, such as by playing against only weak players.

I have asked many people, "How do you define 'winning?'" Their answers are related to their motives on the "Why Do You Play Poker?" questionnaire. Here are just a few of their answers. They want to:

- Become recognized as a top player.
- Win a big tournament.
- Beat their current game for a certain amount.
- Beat a specific, larger game for a certain amount.
- Make enough to live on while living a balanced life.
- End the year ahead a few dollars, but have a lot of fun and never lose so much that it bothers them.
- Just have a good time, while not losing too much money.

This book defines winning in the standard way, "maximizing your long-term profits." If your definition is different, some of its advice may conflict with what *you* want. When my advice conflicts with your priorities, decide whether your priorities are *really* right for you.

I emphasized "really" because most people don't seriously examine their priorities. It's a terrible mistake. As Socrates put it, "An unexamined life is not worth living." If you don't examine your motives, you can make extremely serious errors, not just at poker, but everywhere.

If you seriously examine your motives and decide that your personal definition of winning is different from the standard one of profit maximizing, you should ignore or modify some of my advice.

But understand why you're doing so, and don't pretend that

you're not losing anything. Since you can't avoid trade-offs, make sure that you understand the costs and benefits of various alternatives and then make an informed decision. To put it bluntly, *if you don't know where you want to go, you're probably not going to get there.*

4. Winners Manage Risks and Information Very Well

The key to successful gambling is simply to "get the best of it" and then to "make the most of it."

—**Mason Malmuth**[1]

"Getting the best of it" means discovering or creating situations in which you have an edge, a positive expectation (+EV). "Making the most of it" means acting decisively to get the full value from that edge.

These two steps are easy to describe, but very hard to do. Losers don't perform either one well because:

- They don't get enough information to discover or create an edge.
- They give away information that reduces or eliminates their edge.
- They don't act decisively enough to make the most of it when they have an edge.

Malmuth's quotation is the foundation of this book's organization. Parts 2–5 describe how winners manage risks and information to discover, create, and increase their edge. Part 6 discusses how winners make the most of it by acting decisively.

Many people respond primarily to their emotions instead of managing risks in a controlled, unemotional way. *Risk avoiders* are

---

1. Mason Malmuth, *Gambling Theory and Other Topics* (Henderson, NV: Two Plus Two, 2004), 8.

so afraid of losing that they go to extreme lengths to avoid taking chances, while *risk seekers* take foolish chances to get a "kick."

Instead of responding emotionally, winners avoid both extremes. They realistically analyze the situation, select the strategy that will give them "the best of it," and act decisively to "make the most of it." *If you lack the motivation, discipline, and knowledge to get the best of it or if you lack the decisiveness to make the most of it, you can't become a poker winner.*

The Interdependence of Risk and Information Management

Because poker is an incomplete information game, you can't manage risks properly without managing information well.

You do not need to manage information in chess, checkers, and other complete information games. Every piece is clearly visible on the board, and you know exactly what each piece can do. In poker you cannot see your opponents' cards, nor can they see yours.

The Central Risk-Management Principle

Getting the best of it does *not* mean that you are probably going to succeed. In fact, your chances could be quite slim. There are three critical issues:

1. The probabilities of success and failure
2. The amount at risk
3. The potential payout

The combination of these factors is called expectation, expected value, or just EV. If you already understand this subject, skip the next few paragraphs.

If your EV is negative, you should pass. If it is positive, you should take the risk. "It is often worth taking chances on something that is probably not going to succeed if the rewards compared to the risk or cost compare favorably with the probability of success."[2]

For example, there's an overly simplistic rule: never draw to an inside straight. It's not a bad rule, except for the word "never." That rule is usually valid because the odds against making the straight are about 10 to 1 and the pot usually offers lower odds. However, if you get better odds, you should draw to it. Let's look at the way winners decide whether a risk is worth taking.

Calculating EV

We will deal with a 50:50 risk, but the same principles apply regardless of the probabilities, *if you can financially and psychologically tolerate the risk.*

[EV is] the amount of money that you will win or lose *on average* by making a wager. Say you and a friend agree to bet on the outcome of a coin flip. If the coin lands on heads, he will pay you $1. If it lands on tails, you will pay him $1. Your expectation for this bet is zero. While you will win $1 half the time, you will lose $1 the other half. On average, this bet is break-even.

Let's say your friend decides to pay you $2 for heads, but you still pay only $1 for tails. Now your expectation is fifty cents. . . . On any given flip, you will either win $2 or lose $1. But *on average,* you will win fifty cents per coin flip. Similarly, your friend's expectation is negative fifty cents.

If you make fifty cents per flip, he must lose fifty cents per flip. Money does not appear from nowhere or disappear into nowhere:

2. Mason Malmuth, personal e-mail.

If one person has a positive expectation, another must have a nega-
tive one, and the sum of all expectations must be zero.[3]

Over the long term, EV will be approximately equal to results,
but random variance (aka "luck") will often cause short-term results
to vary considerably from EV. For example, even though betting on
heads with 2-to-1 odds has a large, +EV, tails might come up several
times in a row, causing you to lose.

When flipping coins, there are only two possible outcomes, and
each probability is obvious. In poker you may not know all the possibilities or their exact probabilities. If so, you can't accurately calculate your EV.

EV and Poker

Casinos win, and their customers lose because nearly every bet
is −EV for the customer and +EV for the casino. Only a few poker
players win because the house takes so much in rakes and tips.
They win only because they make *far* more +EV than −EV bets.

Your EV is positive when you are getting better odds from the
pot and future bets than you are paying. If, for example, you have
a 50 percent chance of winning, and the pot and future bets offer
you 4 to 1, you have a large +EV. If you make 100 bets like this, you
expect to be way ahead. All gambling can be reduced to two simple
sentences:

1. If you make enough +EV bets, you *must* win.
2. If you make enough −EV bets, you *must* lose.

3. Ed Miller, David Sklansky, and Mason Malmuth, *Small Stakes Hold'em: Winning
Big with Expert Play* (Henderson, NV: Two Plus Two, 2004), 19f.

If you bet only when you are +EV and don't bet when you are −EV, you *must* eventually win. However, because there are so many unknowns, it is impossible to make only +EV bets. Even the greatest players often misread situations and make −EV bets.

Winners continually strive to make +EV bets.[4] They constantly count the pot, calculate the odds of making their hands, determine the probability that their hand will win, assess the chances that others will fold, check, bet, call, or raise, and consider many other factors. Of course, they make some mistakes, but they are right more often than they are wrong. Once they estimate the EVs, they act decisively.

Losers don't know or don't care about EV, don't bother to make these calculations, or miscalculate. Sometimes they get the best of it, but fail to act decisively enough. Many aggressive losers *appear* to be acting decisively, but they are just gambling foolishly. Decisive action occurs *only* after you have determined that you have the best of it.

The Central Information-Management Principles

Accurately estimating your EV is often difficult, and it's occasionally impossible. You usually can't calculate the exact probabilities and potential gains and losses because you don't know the other players' cards, nor do you know what they'll do.

Risk management depends on information management because:

- The less information you have, the higher your risks and the lower your rewards.

---

4. An exception occurs in cash games and especially tournaments when the +EV bet entails a significant chance of breaking you. Being broke ends your tournament, and in cash games it could prevent you from making future +EV bets.

- The more information your opponents have, the higher your risks and the lower your rewards.

For example, since you don't know your opponents' cards, you can't know whether your hand is better, equal, or worse than theirs. You may not know whether the cards you hope to catch will let you win the pot. And you can rarely be sure of what your opponents will do. Without knowing their cards and thoughts, you can't be sure of your EV. (Slansky puts this all in bold type.)

If everybody's cards were showing at all times, there would always be a precise, mathematically correct play for each player. Any player who deviated from his correct play would be reducing his mathematical expectation and increasing the expectation of his opponents.

Of course, if all cards were exposed at all times, there wouldn't be a game of poker. The art of poker is filling the gaps in the incomplete information provided by your opponents' betting and the exposed cards in open-handed games, and at the same time preventing your opponents from discovering any more than what you want them to know about your hand.

That leads us to the Fundamental Theorem of Poker:

Every time you play a hand differently from the way you would have played it if you could see all your opponents' cards, they gain; and every time you play your hand the same way you would have played it if you could see all their cards, they lose. Conversely, every time opponents play their hands differently from the way they would have played if they could see all your cards, you gain; and every time they play their cards the same way they would have played if they could see all your cards, you lose.[5]

5. David Sklansky, *The Theory of Poker* (Henderson, NV: Two Plus Two, 1999), 17f.

Virtually every significant winner knows and applies that theorem. It is the foundation of all information management. It can be briefly summarized as *the more you know, and the less they know, the lower your risks and the greater your edge.* Therefore, the critical risk/information-management tasks can be simply stated.

1. Learn your opponents' situations and intentions.
2. Conceal your own situation and intentions.

If you perform both tasks well, your risks go down and your rewards go up. For example, if you see that an opponent will fold if you bet, you can easily bluff him. Your superior information management lets you take an apparently risky action without taking any risk!

The law of supply and demand applies to information. If everyone knows certain information, it has hardly any value. If you are the only one who knows it, it can be priceless. Speed is therefore critically important. The sooner you learn something, the more valuable it is. As an extreme example, if you could learn in advance which cards were coming, you would always win. If you can read your opponents faster and better than they can read you, you will usually have the best of it.

More Details About Information Management

Sklansky's theorem and Malmuth's quotation are, I believe, the most important statements ever written about poker. The rest of this book will discuss the ways that winners:

- *Get the best of it* by acquiring more information, processing it well, and transmitting only the information they want opponents to have.
- *Make the most of it* by acting decisively.

The goal of parts 2–5 is to help you create a favorable informa-tion balance by getting more and transmitting less information.

Part 2, "Winners Control Their Focus," states that winners focus on whatever helps them to win, and they ignore or minimize every-thing else. They are so single-minded that poker becomes their en-tire world, at least when they are playing. If something helps them, they will use it. If it does not affect them, they will ignore it. If it harms them, they will avoid it. Losers do not focus nearly as well. Their attention drifts from subject to subject, and they waste time and energy on irrelevancies.

Part 3, "Winners Control Their Thought Processes," states that winners and losers don't just focus on different subjects. They think in very different ways. It doesn't matter what information you get if you don't process it correctly. Losers think badly because they don't want to work hard, and they want to preserve their cher-ished illusions about poker and themselves. Winners have the dis-cipline to work hard, they want to know the truth, and they think in ways that help to discover it.

Part 4, "Winners Control the Information They Transmit," dis-cusses the second half of The Fundamental Theorem of Poker, de-ceiving your opponents. Since deceptive actions normally reduce your short-term EV, you must ensure that you pay less now than you gain later. One cost that winners minimize, but losers over-value is their opponents' feelings about them. Winners make de-ceptive moves and create images that cost them affection or even respect, but get the best long-term results.

Part 5, "Winners Control Their Reactions to Feelings," is a transi-tion between getting the best of it by managing information and making the most of it by acting decisively. You need to control your emotional reactions to perform both tasks well. Poor emotional control has destroyed many talented players, and good control has helped many less gifted players to win consistently.

Accepting responsibility for your own results is the foundation of good control. Losers blame bad luck, mistakes by dealers and other players, unfair rules, and many other factors to protect their egos by rejecting this responsibility. Winners accept responsibility, and it helps them stay in control.

You Must Act Decisively

Parts 2–5 tell you how to get an edge. but *that edge will accomplish little unless you exploit it by acting DECISIVELY.*

The word "decisive" was emphasized because you can't fully exploit your edge without being decisive. The ability to exploit edges is almost independent of the ability to get them. Some losers know what to do, but don't do it.

Unfortunately, no matter how well you manage information, nearly all poker decisions must be made with incomplete information. Some risk seekers don't care; instead of trying to get enough information, they just act impulsively. Some risk avoiders say, "Don't make a decision until you get all the facts," but you'll hardly ever get them all. This position is often just an excuse for indecisiveness.

Whether you like it or not, you *must* make your decisions quickly with incomplete information. You can't stall, procrastinate, or form a study committee. When it's your turn to act, you must put in your money or fold your cards.

Indecisive players often choose the "safest" option, checking or calling, rather than betting or raising. These actions seem to minimize risk, but they will often increase it. The small amount they save by not betting or raising can cost them a whole pot.

Winners accept that decisions *must* be made without complete information, but they definitely don't act impulsively. They do everything they can to obtain the information they need, to get the best of it, and then they act decisively to make the most of it.

But What About Luck?

Forget about it. Nothing you can do will affect it, and over the long term it usually evens out. This book focuses on the only things you can control: your own thoughts, feelings, and actions because they determine whether you get the best of it and make the most of it.

- If you control them, you will win.
- If you waste your time and energy trying to control luck, you will lose.

David Sklansky and Mason Malmuth put luck into the proper perspective. The final words of their book were, "We wish you 'average luck.' That's all you will need if you have been paying attention."[6]

Winners' Laws

This chapter has four Winners' Laws, and they are very general. The remaining chapters will spell out the specific actions you should take to apply them.

1. Do whatever it takes to get the best of it.
2. Get as much information as possible.

---

6. David Sklansky and Mason Malmuth, *How to Make $100,000 a Year Gambling for a Living* (Henderson, NV: Two Plus Two, 1997), 284.

3. Give away as little information as possible.
4. When you get the best of it, act decisively to make the most of it.

How Do You Rate?

This chapter covers managing risks and information, but we will rate only risk management now. In parts 2 through 5 you will rate yourself on many information-management skills.

Circle the number that best describes your agreement with this statement: *I am neither a risk seeker nor a risk avoider. While playing poker, I always try to get the best of it and to make the most of it.* (7) Agree strongly, (6) Agree, (5) Agree somewhat, (4) Neutral, (3) Disagree somewhat, (2) Disagree, (1) Disagree strongly.

Circle that number in the appropriate place on page 262.

The Critical Questions

Review this chapter, especially the Winners' Laws and How Do You Rate? sections. Then answer two questions:

1. What are the implications of my self-rating?
2. What should I do differently? List *specific actions* you should take to improve your risk management.

Discuss your answers with someone you trust and take good notes.

Winners Control Their Focus

Introduction: Winners Control Their Focus

Most poker writers emphasize processing information such as memorizing the odds and understanding the meaning of various bets and tells. They pay much less attention to acquiring information, but it's at least as important. If you don't get the right information, what you know or how well you think don't matter much.

Part 2 discusses the way winners control their focus to get the right information, while part 3 discusses how they process it. This distinction is somewhat blurred. The way winners focus affects the way they process information and vice versa.

Your motives and focus overlap. You naturally focus on what you want. However, if you don't understand how various factors affect each other or if you lack discipline, you may focus on the wrong subjects. For example, you may want to increase your long-term profits but focus frequently on subjects that reduce it.

Since winners want to maximize their edge, they focus on topics that increase it, and they pay little attention to everything else. Losers don't control their focus, wasting time and energy on subjects that don't affect profits.

First and most important, winners focus on *long-term results* (profits) because they are the way we keep score. They are the primary, almost the only criterion, of success, making them the winners' central focus. They minimize almost everything else, such as a love of action, a desire to impress people, bad beats, lucky breaks, and winning or losing streaks.

Since their long-term profits will be approximately equal to the total EV of their decisions, they focus on making good decisions. They will even make short-term sacrifices of chips, time, and comfort to increase their ultimate profits. For example, they invest time and money in developing their skills and deliberately misplay occasional hands to create an image or set a trap.

Despite their long-term focus, they remain firmly grounded in the present. Instead of worrying about the past or dreaming of the future, they focus on the *here and now.* They constantly ask themselves, To maximize my EV, what must I do *now*?

Because poker is a power-oriented, predatory game, winners focus on *power* and minimize luck, justice, fairness, and personal relationships. They are constantly assessing everyone's power, trying to get more of it, and deferring actions until the power balance favors them.

Since power is always relative, winners naturally focus on *other people.* They constantly compare their opponents' cards, skills, and styles to their own. They also try to understand their opponents' motives, thoughts, and attitudes. Why are they acting this way? What do they want? How do they think? How can I get them to do what I want?

Because trying to focus on so many subjects is confusing, losers often oversimplify poker. They want a simple formula or a short list of do's and don'ts. Winners reject such simplifications and *consider complexities.* They know that there are no simple formulas and that the right strategy depends on the situation. They ignore the attractively simplistic world of the losers and consider poker's complex realities.

5. Winners Focus on Long-Term Results

If you can't win, lose, just as long as you keep playing.
— **Nick "The Greek" Dandolos**[1]

You can't win every game. . . . You must think of your wins at the end of the year.
— **David Sklansky**[2]

These two quotations summarize this chapter's central principle. Nick "The Greek" Dandolos was a loser, but he was inducted into the Poker Hall of Fame. He is famous primarily for losing a highly publicized series of head-to-head matches against Johnny Moss, his era's greatest player. Nobody knows exactly how much he lost then, but some estimates range from $2 to $4 million.

"Near the end of his life Dandolos was near broke and playing $5 limit draw poker games in Gardena, California. When asked by a fellow player how he could once play for millions and now be playing for such small stakes, Dandolos supposedly replied, 'Hey, it's action, isn't it?'"[3]

He was an excellent player, but his love for action destroyed him. His life epitomized the dangers of focusing on anything but results. But you should also ask, "What kind of results?"

David Sklansky repeatedly answered that question. You must

1. Nick made similar statements many times.

2. David Sklansky, *The Theory of Poker* (Henderson, NV: Two Plus Two, 1999), p. 6.

3. en.wikipedia.org/wiki/Nick_the_Greek

think of *long-term* results. If you focus on action or short-term results, you will probably end up broke, just like Nick "The Greek."

The Dangers of Focusing on Anything but Results

There are many action lovers like Nick at every level, from tiny stakes to enormous ones. For example, many no-hopers enter the biggest tournaments for the kick of playing in them. Winners call them "dead money." Since the prize pool comes from entry fees, this dead money is their primary source of profits. Without dead money, many pros would avoid tournaments because they can't win much from each other.

Although so few people win, cardroom and online poker are flourishing. The losers pay the winners and the house billions of dollars every year. They do it for the kick of gambling, the experience of challenging better players, the fun of socializing, and a host of other reasons. Regardless of their reasons, not focusing on results virtually guarantees losing.

Winners focus on results because they are intense competitors, and poker success is measured very simply. Results are the *only* thing that counts.

You get no points for style, grace, knowledge, or anything else. A loser may feel good about winning luckily or outplaying a better player. Winners ignore these pleasures because they know that the scoring system is very simple. If I am a nicer guy, know more theory, make fancier plays, and tell better stories, but you end up with more money, you're a better player, period, end of story.

Their commitment and focus make winners subordinate everything else to winning. If something doesn't affect their long term results, they ignore it. It would be more pleasant to relax, gamble for fun, and focus on other things, but they sacrifice these pleasures to maximize their profits.

The Dangers of Focusing on Short-Term Results

Focusing on short-term results is the natural thing to do. Psychological research proves that short-term rewards and punishments have much greater effects on feelings and behavior than longer-term ones.

Because luck has such huge effects, winners know that short-term results can be extremely misleading. A good decision can cost them money, whereas a bad one can yield a profit. You must therefore look beyond the immediate results and focus on every decision's longer-term consequences.

It is a fundamental premise of the game that you must make correct decisions and not concern yourself with consequences. . . . Whether you are right or wrong in the current situation makes no difference. What matters is that your judgments are sound, based on the best information available to you. If your judgments are better in the long run than those of your opponents, you will be taking home the money in the long run.[4]

Losers react to impulses—including quite foolish ones—then feel vindicated if they get lucky. The immediate kick prevents them from seeing that their decision-making process *guarantees* that they will be long-term losers.

For example, a loser may foolishly play weak cards, get lucky,

---

4. Roy Cooke, "Judgment Bet/Judgment Check," *Card Player*, September 18, 1998, 104.

and win a huge pot. Instead of recognizing his mistake, he may congratulate himself for being brilliant, intuitive, or courageous. Of course, people who play terrible cards will certainly be long-term losers, but they may look very good for a little while. They may even feel contempt for the "cowardly" or "unimaginative" people who play the percentages, study strategy, and wait for good cards.

Expected Value Equals Long-Term Profit

Poker winners focus on maximizing their long-term expected value (EV). They know that their long-term results will be close to their EV and that making negative EV plays will ultimately be disastrous.

Winners apply the same general principles as casinos. Their operators actually want people to win huge jackpots or get hot at the crap tables. When someone wins big, an operator puts his name and picture on billboards or television. Those rare, highly publicized wins bring in more suckers, and casino managers know that—because the odds favor them—the more money people bet, the more the house *must* win.

Poker winners think the same way. When suckers make a bad play and get lucky, the suckers get a huge kick. Winners don't correct their reasoning. Instead, they say, "Well played!" or "You really have a lot of courage." Winners want suckers to keep making –EV plays because their bad decisions increase the winners' EV and long-term profits.

They constantly think in terms of EV. They would like to win this hand, of course, but winning it is much less important than maximizing their EV. If they can get a favorable expectation, they know they must ultimately win.

Mathematical expectation has nothing to do with [short-term] results. The imbecile [who makes a foolish bet] might win the first ten in a row, but . . . it makes no difference whether you win or lose a certain bet or series of bets. . . . If you continue to make these [+EV] bets, you will win.[5]

The central feature of the professional attitude [is]: *The awareness of the need to focus, not on short-term results, but on the quality of your play.*[6]

Losers dream of getting lucky and making brilliant moves, but poker rewards disciplined, +EV play. The courageous (actually foolhardy) gamble that wins against the odds may make your heart pound and other players applaud, but those plays don't improve your bottom line. It's another case of the tortoise defeating the hare. The steady players end up with the money. Most profits come from other people's mistakes, not brilliant moves, and certainly not from –EV plays.

I Play Too Well to Beat These Idiots

Countless losers have this silly belief, and they express it in many different ways:

- "I'd rather play against good players than bad ones."
- "I'm moving to bigger games so that people will respect my bets and raises."
- "That game is 'too good to beat.' "

---

5. Sklansky, *Theory of Poker*, 9.

6. John Feeney, *Inside the Poker Mind* (Henderson, NV, Two Plus Two, 2000) 222. The italics were in the text.

- *"Nobody* can beat that game because they call with any-thing."
- "No matter how well I play, somebody always draws out on me."

No matter how that belief is expressed, it is utter, absolute non-sense. It is *much* easier to beat weak players than strong ones, and you gain from every one of your opponents' –EV plays. However, you must adjust to the way *these* opponents play. If you try to bluff calling stations or make subtle moves on clueless players, you will lose, *and you will deserve to lose.*

These beliefs and complaints are based on short-term frustra-tions, not long-term EV. It is frustrating to have suckers draw out on you, and the more suckers in a game, the more often it will hap-pen. However, winners know that they will be paid very well for that frustration because their profits *increase* when people play bad cards.[7]

So stop kidding yourself. Every time your opponents make –EV plays, they *increase* your EV and long-term profits. *"If you do not win in the long run, it is not because your opponents are making too many mistakes; it is because you are."*[8]

Subtler Short-Term Satisfactions

Some losers commit another type of shortsighted stupidity. They criticize opponents for making mistakes. For example, if

---

7. If you have any doubts, re-read the discussion of Situation A in appendix A. It shows that pocket aces are most profitable against nine opponents with ran-dom cards.

8. Ed Miller, David Sklansky, and Mason Malmuth, *Small Stakes Hold'em: Winning Big Through Expert Play* (Henderson, NV: Two Plus Two, 2004) 18. Italics are in the book.

someone wins a pot with a miracle card, a loser might say, "That was really stupid. The odds against catching it were 22:1, and you were getting only 4:1."

He gets the short-term satisfaction of expressing his frustration and perhaps impressing or getting sympathy from other players. But the long-term impact is quite negative. First, he educates his opponents, making them harder to beat. Second, he may embarrass weak players, causing them to play better, move to another table, go home, or even stop playing poker.

A key part of a long-term focus is making short-term sacrifices of other satisfactions. For example, you may start by playing very aggressively to create the impression that you're a wild player and then take advantage of that image by playing very conservatively. Chapters 16 and 17 will tell you when and how to be deceptive. Now I will just give an example I read over forty years ago, but never forgot.

Oswald Jacoby, a great bridge and poker player, once put chips on his hole card every time it was an ace in five-card stud. After his opponents had spotted it, he stopped doing it, and he even folded a few times (which cost him money) to preserve the illusion. Finally, he had one ace up and one in the hole. After waiting until all the cards had been dealt and knowing that his hand was unbeatable, he pushed in his stack. His opponent was sure Jacoby was bluffing and called. The small cost of setting the trap earned him a huge profit.

Personal Development

"Although they focus on the long term when discussing how to play hands, many poker writers have a short-term, narrow focus. They concentrate on how to play hands, not on your long-term personal development."[9]

9. Alan Schoonmaker, *Your Best Poker Friend,* (NY: Lyle Stuart, 2007), 231.

In order to develop your skills, you will often have to *reduce* your short-term profits or even (gasp) take some losses. Every hour you spend studying or preparing in other ways obviously costs you the money you could win by playing. You can win the most by playing in soft games, but if you always do so, you won't develop the skills you need to move up and win more money.

Barry Tanenbaum agrees. He once played heads-up against a world-famous player. When I asked why he would take such a "foolish" gamble, he said, "I could learn something, and what I learned might make me more profit in the future." He said that always trying for the maximum EV was the same as a "company's maximizing short-term profits by eliminating its R&D department."

Barry is a long-term winner and highly respected writer. Follow his lead and think of the *real* long term. Play to maximize your EV, but also invest the time, energy, and money to maximize your *lifetime's* profits.[10]

Winners' Laws

These laws will help you to shift your focus from short-term satisfactions to the broader, longer-term picture.

1. Ask yourself constantly: Am I focusing on long-term results or short-term satisfactions?

If you don't ask that question, the natural tendency to emphasize short-term rewards and punishments will distract you from focusing on your long-term EV. You will make mistakes for emotional

---

10. But beware of rationalizing. You may play in larger games or against tougher players because you want the kick of gambling or need to prove something. Then you may rationalize that you were really trying to develop your skills. You must analyze your own motives *honestly*.

or careless reasons and may not make necessary investments in your self-development.

2. Emphasize making good decisions, and minimize short-term results.

If you focus too much on short-term results, you'll distract yourself from the important issue: did you make the right decision?

If the answer is yes, don't worry about the results. If the answer is no, work on your decision-making skills.

3. Record your wins and losses accurately.

If you do not write down every chip you buy and cash in, you will probably delude yourself about your long-term results. You will "forget" how many chips you bought or ignore some losses. You may even make excuses such as, "I did not write down last night's loss because I was drinking, terribly unlucky, distracted by a family problem," and so on.

Without accurate records you will probably make bad decisions. For example, you may not know that you lose in certain games. If you enjoy those games, you will keep playing in them.

Accurate records will also help you to cope with bad beats, losing sessions, and losing streaks. Comparing them to your total wins or losses will show you that they don't matter that much.

4. Minimize everything else and focus on whatever improves your long-term results.

You may object that this narrow focus is unbalanced and unhealthy. I agree, but—as I said earlier—this book is about winning, not mental health or lifestyles. The biggest winners are not balanced. *To be a big winner, you must focus on your long-term results.*

How Do You Rate?

This rating scale assesses your tendency to focus on the long-term results or short-term rewards and punishments.

Circle the number that best describes your agreement with this statement: *While playing poker, I am extremely focused on long-term results. I nearly ignore short-term rewards and punishments.* (7) Agree strongly, (6) Agree, (5) Agree somewhat, (4) Neutral, (3) Disagree somewhat, (2) Disagree, (1) Disagree strongly.

Circle that number in the appropriate place on page 262.

The Critical Questions

Review this chapter, especially the Winners' Laws and How Do You Rate? sections. Then answer two questions:

1. What are the implications of my self-rating?
2. What should I do differently? List *specific actions* you should take to improve your focus on long-term results.

Discuss your answers with someone you trust and take good notes.

6. Winners Focus on the Here and Now

At a poker table you get paid only for making the right decision now.

—**Barry Tanenbaum**[1]

This chapter's title may seem to contradict the last one's, but there is no real contradiction. To maximize your long-term profits, you must focus on the critical question: What should I do now?

Barry Tanenbaum expanded his comment: "Forget about whether you are winning or losing and what happened in the last hand. If you make the right decision *now,* you must ultimately win."

Dr. John Feeney, a psychologist, agrees: "Most players are too focused on winning. It is far more productive to make correct play your goal and let winning take care of itself."[2]

An Illustration

Let's take two cases:

1. You're playing no-limit hold'em.
2. The pot is $100.
3. You will win if you catch the right card and lose if you don't.
4. You will know the exact odds against catching it.

1. Barry Tanenbaum, personal conversation with author, July 15, 2004.

2. John Feeney, *Inside the Poker Mind* (Henderson, NV: Two Plus Two, 2000) 298.

5. You have no more betting because the bettor is all in.
6. You are even for the night and have $200 worth of chips.

Case A: The odds against catching your card are 10:1. You have invested $30 in the pot, and it will cost you another $15 to call the last bet.

Case B: The odds against catching your card are 4:1. You have invested $20 in the pot, and it will cost you another $20 to call the last bet.

In which case would you be more likely to call?

Would you make a different decision if you were winning $500? Losing $500?

Write your answers before looking at the answer opposite.

_____

_____

_____

Answer

You can't draw firm conclusions from only two answers, but they do suggest something about your thinking.

- If you answered Case A, you were thinking like a loser.
- If you answered Case B, you were thinking like a winner. You should see whether this pattern occurs in other places.

Case A has a negative expectation. The odds against winning are 10:1, but you are getting only 6.67:1 ($100/$15 = 6.67). If you do it 110 times, you will have:

Win $100 10 times	= +$1,000
Lose $15 100 times	= –$1,500
Net loss for 110 times	= $500
Average loss per bet	= $4.54 (about 30% of the $15 bet)

Case B has a positive expectation. The odds against winning are 4:1, but you are getting 5:1 ($100/$20 = 5). If you do it 100 times, you will have:

Win $100 20 times	= +$2,000
Lose $20 80 times	= –$1,600
Net gain for 100 times	= $400
Average gain per bet	= $4 (20% of the $20 bet)

Ignore Irrelevant Factors

But what about the difference in your investment? Isn't risking another $15 to protect a $30 investment better than risking $20 to protect a $20 investment? The answer could not be simpler: No no no!

Once you put a dollar in the pot, it isn't yours anymore. It's the same as every other dollar in there. Winners don't think of "protecting their investments." Instead, they base their decisions on their expectation *now.*

What about the way you're running? Should you decide differently if you are winning or losing? Again, the answer is no! Your past results are irrelevant, and winners ignore them and other irrelevancies such as how lucky they feel. If the expectation *now* is positive, they bet. If the expectation *now* is negative, they pass. If they do it enough times, they must win.

Many losers can't think that way. For example, they say to themselves, "I've gone this far, so I've got to call." Or "I haven't made a flush all night, and I'm due." Or "I'm so hot that I know my card is coming." All these statements are dumb.

Deciding Whether to Play or Quit

An even dumber statement is, "I've *got* to get even." If you think that way, you will probably play badly. Instead of rationally assessing your current expectation, you will focus on your feelings. Desperate attempts to get even have wiped out countless bankrolls.

Since the past is irrelevant, you should base your play or quit decision *entirely* on your expectation *now.* "You should not allow the fact that you are winning or losing to affect your decision to stay or quit a game. From a money-making point of view the only criterion for playing is whether you are a favorite or an underdog."[3]

Some stay-or-quit rules are silly: "Quit when you are ahead." "Quit when you have doubled or tripled your investment."

3. David Sklansky, *The Theory of Poker* (Henderson, NV: Two Plus Two, 1999), 7.

On the other hand, quitting when you have lost a certain amount (such as two or three buy-ins) is quite reasonable. If you lose too much, you may think, "I've got to get even," and play poorly.

In addition, winning may suggest that you have an edge in this game, and losing may suggest the opposite. Perhaps you're playing better or worse than usual or your results may have affected your table image and your opponents' reactions. Consider all these factors, and then base your play-or-quit decision *entirely* on your expectation *now*.

Coin Flips

If an honest coin comes up heads ten consecutive times, what are the odds on heads the next flip?

They are exactly the same as any other time, 50:50. A coin has no memory, and previous flips have no influence on this one. Suckers have lost *billions* of dollars using silly systems that ignore that reality. The most common is doubling their bets every time they lose an approximately even money bet such as red/black in roulette. They think that red must ultimately hit, and when it does, they will be ahead for the entire series.

True, red will certainly come up, and when it does, they will be ahead. However, each bet is –EV because the green 0 and (on some wheels) 00 make the actual odds slightly worse than even money. Because each bet is –EV, the entire series must also be –EV.

If they play this system long enough, they must go broke. Occasionally, black comes up 13 or 16 or even 25 times in a row. Even with a million-dollar bankroll and a casino without betting limits, that system guarantees that you will go broke, as countless fools have already learned.

Winners never play roulette, craps, and similar games because it is impossible to beat them. Surprisingly, some of the world's greatest poker players are often broke because they can't keep away from these games. That weakness is one reason for my saying that winning is somewhat unrelated to talent. There are supremely talented losers and modestly talented winners.

Don't Play "Woulda, Coulda, Shoulda" Games

Some losers watch the action, not to learn from it, but to second-guess their past decisions. Then, instead of focusing on how to play this hand, they mentally replay past hands. "I should have cold-called that raise with my seven-five of hearts, I would have made a flush. I would have won $142, and I'd be ahead $25 instead of down $117."

When winners fold a hand, they mentally erase it—unless they can learn from it. They can't have those cards back, so they forget them and focus on what they should do *now*: play their best and gather information to make future adjustments.

Don't Dream About the Future

Winners *plan* for the future. They think about how they should play this and future hands. Losers *dream* about the future. "If I win this pot, I will be down only $130. Then I will just need one more to be even for the night."

While losers are brooding about the past and dreaming of the future, winners study the other players and decide how to adjust their strategy. It's the smartest thing they can do at the most important time—*now*.

Winners' Laws

1. Keep focused on what you should do *now* to maximize your long-term profits.

Don't worry about the past or dream about the future. Concentrate on what you should do *now*.

2. Accept that lost money, time, and effort are gone forever.

They are like the money in the pot. It doesn't matter who put it in; what matters is who takes it out. Invest your money and time *only* when you can profit from it.

3. Pay attention to what you are thinking.

Constantly ask yourself, Am I focused on my current expectation or am I thinking about something else?

How Do You Rate?

This rating scale measures how much you focus on the here and now, the decision at hand versus the past, future, and other irrelevant factors.

Circle the number that best describes your agreement with this statement: *While playing poker, I focus completely on what I must do **here and now** to get the best long-term results.* (7) Agree strongly, (6) Agree, (5) Agree somewhat, (4) Neutral, (3) Disagree somewhat, (2) Disagree, (1) Disagree strongly.

Circle that number in the appropriate place on page 262.

The Critical Questions

Review this chapter, especially the Winners' Laws and How Do You Rate? sections. Then answer two questions:

1. What are the implications of my self-rating?
2. What should I do differently? List *specific actions* you should take to improve your focus on the here and now.

Discuss your answers with someone you trust and take good notes.

7. Winners Focus on Power

*Poker is all about picking on the weak. It may be weak
hands, weak players, or just weak play.*

> —**Barry Shulman,** CEO of *Card Player*'s
> parent corporation[1]

You may dislike Barry Shulman's position because picking on the weak seems immoral, and it's certainly not chivalrous. If it bothers you, poker may be the wrong game for you, but Barry accurately described its essential nature. It's predatory, but so is life in general. The strong eat the weak *everywhere,* not just at the poker table. Winners recognize that reality, while losers deny, minimize, or ignore it.

Because they are so competitive and realistic, winners focus on power, not luck, justice, morality, personal relationships, or fairness. Poker and life are "unfair." The best poker player doesn't always win, nor does the one who "deserves" it for other reasons. Cancer, traffic accidents, and other tragedies happen to wonderful people, while drunken wife beaters win the lottery. That's the way poker and life are, and you should accept and cope with that painful reality.

Winners constantly strive to increase their power, aka their edge. They want the best seat in the best game, and they wait until they have the right cards and situation. Your edge shifts constantly. You may have had an edge moments ago, but it can disappear immediately. Winners always want to know how strong their position is *now.*

1. Barry Shulman, "Shulman Says," *Card Player,* October 24, 2003, 10.

Despite its importance, many people ignore or minimize power because they believe that it shouldn't be so important. They focus on more pleasant subjects, such as luck, morality, and personal relationships. Doing so makes them more comfortable, but costs them chips.

Because it focused on how to acquire and use power, *The Prince* is regarded as an evil book, and "Machiavellian" means "duplicitous," "deceitful," or just plain "evil." This perception shows how uncomfortable people are with power. An ideal world would be run by moralists, but our world is run by power-oriented people. In fact, many of history's most powerful men studied *The Prince,* and I urge you to read it.

David Apostolico has written an excellent book, *Machiavellian Poker Strategy.*[2] He convincingly argues that people who accept and utilize Machiavelli's emphasis on power and realism are much more likely to win at the poker table and elsewhere.

When you're playing poker, power overwhelms justice, fairness, and all the other factors that most people hold dear. Let's say you have lost all your money, maxed out your credit cards, borrowed from everyone possible, and can't pay your overdue rent tomorrow. If you lose this pot, you'll be in big trouble. You're playing seven-card stud against a drunken millionaire who doesn't care about the money.

Your first three cards are all aces, the best possible hand, while your only opponent has absolute trash. He should fold, but he hangs around, catches four cards to make a straight, and takes your last dollar. If poker were based on fairness or justice, you would have won the pot and paid your rent. But since a straight is more

2. David Apostolico, *Machiavellian Poker Strategy* (NY: Kensington, 2005).

powerful than three aces, you're broke and in danger of being evicted.

You should accept that people who rely on justice, truth, morals, luck, or just about anything but power are "natural victims." Denying power's importance just increases the power-oriented people's edge over you.

Power Is Always Relative, Not Absolute

Your power depends on the relationship between your cards, skills, position, and so on, and those of the other people. This relativity is most obvious in the way pots are awarded.

In real life power is often confusing. The "slam dunk" lawsuit loses when the jury ignores the evidence. A great product is so ahead of its time that it fails in the marketplace. The best runner stumbles on the track. That uncertainty is not true in poker. If the cards are shown down, a flush *always* beats a straight; three deuces *always* beat aces and kings.

A full house of aces over kings is a great hand, but—if someone has quads—it will cost you a bundle because you will raise and reraise. Conversely, a pair of deuces is a bad hand, unless your opponents have worse ones.

Since only one hand can win each pot, every reasonably competent player constantly asks the critical question, *Is my hand the strongest?* If it is not, do the odds of its becoming the strongest hand (plus the odds of bluffing successfully) justify making a bet? You can't play poker for long without realizing power's importance. *The entire game is based on the power relationship between hands.*

Skill and Discipline Are the Most Enduring Power Sources

If you don't play better than your opposition, you must ultimately lose. In fact, since the house takes so much money, you must be *much* better to win.[3] If nobody has a significant edge, you all lose.

Winners recognize this fact and constantly compare themselves to the other players. Selecting games with the right kinds of weaker players has more impact on your results than anything else, perhaps more than all the other factors combined. Yet many losers pay little attention to this crucial issue. In fact, some people deliberately seek tough games to get a kick. If you really care more about that kick than money, it's OK to seek tough games. But, if you want to be a winner, it's self-destructive.

Your Bankroll Is a Major Source of Power

If you play above your bankroll, you are taking a terrible risk. First, a run of bad luck can bust you. Second, you will probably play "scared," and scared play is bad play.

Let's look again at going broke with three aces. You may protest that your aces gave you the power, but you still lost, that luck overwhelmed power. Sure, your hand would usually win, but you had weakened yourself by neglecting a critically important source of power, your bankroll. Winners do their best to avoid such weak positions. Since their skill will ultimately prevail, but horrendous luck is part of the game, they make sure that they have enough money to survive the inevitable losing streaks.

3. You need a much larger edge in smaller games because the house's charges are relatively higher.

Many full-time pros have gone broke repeatedly. They may blame bad luck, but unrealistic thinking about bankrolls has often been a major factor. "One of the things that has been the downfall of many professional gamblers is that they are underbankrolled."[4] Winners make sure that they have adequate capital for *this* game. If their bankroll becomes too small for their usual game, they play for lower stakes to ensure survival.

Position Is a Major Source of Power

The earlier you must act, the weaker you are. You do not know what the players behind you will do, and they will know what you have done before acting. Position is always important, but its effect and value depend on your opposition.

Let's see how position affects the way a winner would play a pair of fives before the flop in hold'em. Unless he catches a third five, he has little chance of winning against more than one opponent.[5] If he doesn't flop it, he'll usually fold because the odds against catching it later are too high. Because the odds against flopping it are about 7.5 to 1, he wants to see the flop cheaply and to have a large field so that he gets high odds and will be paid off if he flops it.

First Situation

He is under the gun, a weak position. Against weak, loose, passive players, he would probably *call* because he could expect several calls and no raises. If he flopped a set, he could play aggressively,

---

4. David Sklansky and Mason Malmuth, *Gambling for a Living* (Henderson, NV: Two Plus Two, 1997), 277.

5. He might use the power of late position to play this hand aggressively against one weak limper or the blinds, but I won't discuss this situation.

confident that he would get paid off. If the flop missed him, he could fold cheaply.

Second Situation

He is again under the gun, but his opponents are strong, tight, and aggressive. He would usually *fold*. He could not expect many callers, and somebody would probably raise. It would cost him more to try to catch that five, and if he caught it, he would be much less likely to be paid off. He would also have poor position after the flop against strong players.

Third Situation

He is on the button, and six weak, passive players have called. Now he would probably raise. He is getting good odds to flop a set, the competition is weak, and he will always have the best position. He might also get a "four-card flop" because these players almost automatically "check to the raiser." His cards are the same, but—because of different positions and opponents—his power and decisions are completely different.

Position is so important that you will be a lifetime loser to the people on your immediate left, but a lifetime winner from the ones on your immediate right. Winners always try for the seat that gives them the best position. They try to sit to the right of passive, predictable players and to the left of aggressive, unpredictable ones. If the only seat available is in a bad position, they might not even join a game. They do not want aggressive, unpredictable players to have position on them.

Some Kinds of Power Change Frequently

In flop games position changes every hand, and in stud it can change with every card.

Every card can change the power balance. The losing flush draw is suddenly unbeatable when the fifth spade hits. You obviously have to understand and adjust to this huge change.

Every bet can cause winners to re-assess the power balance. They thought Charlie had a weak hand, but he just made a big raise. They must immediately analyze why he did it and then react appropriately. Winners do it automatically, while some losers may ignore this information. They play their own cards almost without regard to the other players' cards and actions.

Winners also know which conditions affect their power. For example, a very tight player will beat a ten-handed loose-passive game, but will have little chance in an aggressive five-handed one. Winners know where their style fits and then either adapt it or quit when conditions change.

Winners avoid the tougher players and attack the weaker ones. They also know that the combination of styles—the "chemistry" between players—affects the power balance. In poker, as in sports, player A may have the edge over player B; player B may have the edge over player C; but player C has the edge over player A. If they don't have the edge over *this* player, they avoid him.

Winners' Laws

1. Emphasize power, not luck, justice, or morality.

Since poker is based on power, you have to get in step with reality. Don't waste your time worrying about luck, justice, or fairness, and *don't* expect sympathy. If you whine about luck and tell bad beat stories, you'll weaken yourself in two ways: First, you tell opponents how you think and play, and the smart ones will use that information against you. Second, you will appear to be a weak whiner, and tough players will exploit your weakness to upset you further and put you on tilt.

2. Constantly assess the power balance.

Because it changes so frequently, repeatedly ask: How powerful am I? How powerful are other people? What is the basis of my power? What about theirs?

3. Constantly strive to become stronger.

Keep looking for ways to increase your edge. Winners constantly look for the softer game, the better seat, the easier opponent.

4. Adjust your strategy to fit your power position.

When you've got power, use it. Play more hands and play them more aggressively.

When you're weak, be cautious. Wait until you're stronger. If you can't become stronger, change games or go home.

How Do You Rate?

This rating scale measures the degree to which you focus on power or on "nicer" subjects, such as moral principles, luck, personal relationships, or fairness.

Circle the number that best describes your agreement with this statement: *While playing poker, I focus entirely on power and ignore luck, morality, personal relationships, and so on.* (7) Agree strongly, (6) Agree, (5) Agree somewhat, (4) Neutral, (3) Disagree somewhat, (2) Disagree, (1) Disagree strongly.

Circle that number in the appropriate place on page 262.

Winners Control Their Focus   83

The Critical Questions

Review this chapter, especially the Winners' Laws and How Do You Rate? sections. Then answer two questions:

1. What are the implications of my self-rating?
2. What should I do differently? List *specific actions* you should take to improve your focus on power.

Discuss your answers with someone you trust and take good notes.

8. Winners Focus on Other People

Don't just play your cards; play your people.
— **Doyle Brunson,** member, Poker Hall of Fame[1]

Doyle is an immortal partly *because* he focuses on other people. He knows that you can't win without focusing on them. We see again how unnaturally winners act. Is it natural to focus on yourself? Of course it is, but it is also natural to lose. Never forget that only a few players win, and they win because they act unnaturally.

Since your power depends on how your cards, skill, position, and so on, compare to those of the other players, you have to focus on them. The information you should get about them can be divided into three time periods: short term, long term, and intermediate term.

Short-Term Information

The most important short-term information is the other players' cards and intentions. What do they have? What do they intend to do? Winners work very hard to get this information, while some losers ignore it.

---

1. Doyle "Texas Dolly" Brunson, *According to Doyle (Poker Wisdom from the World Champion)* (Gambling Times Books, 1984) 7. Distributed by Lyle Stuart, Seacaucus, NJ.

Their Cards

David Sklansky wrote: "The ability to read hands may be the most important weapon a poker player can have."[2] Despite its importance, many losers focus on their own cards and don't seriously try to read their opponents' hands. When they have a good hand, they fall in love with it, betting and raising, even when someone obviously has a better one. With a bad hand they get angry or look disgustedly at it, inviting someone to bluff with an even worse one.

You can read cards by opponents' betting patterns and tells, and both require focusing on your opponents.

- "The most common way to read hands is to analyze the meaning of an opponent's check, bet, or raise, and then to consider the plays he has made throughout the hand, along with the exposed cards."[3]
- "Any mannerism which helps you determine the secrets of an opponent's hand is called a *tell*."[4]

Their Intentions

Many losers don't look at their opponents, or they look to their right to see what opponents have done. Winners look left to learn the intentions of the people *behind* them. They apply a simple principle: *the earlier information is received and the fewer people who have it, the more valuable it is.*

Many opponents telegraph their intentions. They may be ready

2. David Sklansky, *The Theory of Poker* (Henderson, NV: Two Plus Two, 1999) 221.

3. Mason Malmuth, "Five Skills to Work On," *Poker Essays,* vol. 3 (Henderson, NV: Two Plus Two, 2001) 42.

4. Mike Caro, *The Body Language of Poker* (Secaucus, NJ: Caro Publishing Group, 1984) xvii.

to fold their cards or have chips in their hand, ready to bet or raise. They may even take the exact number that they intend to bet. Or they may send subtler signals such as absentmindedly shuffling their cards or ignoring the action. If you know their intentions, you can make much better decisions.

Long-Term Information

The most important long-term information is the comparison between your skills and style and those of your opponents. If you are stronger and have the right style, you have an edge and vice versa.

Winners also study opponents to learn their motives, thoughts, and attitudes. What do they want? How do they think? Why are they acting this way? How can I get them to do what I want? To accomplish these formidable tasks, many winners keep mental or written "books" on other players the way baseball catchers keep books on hitters.

> In top-class poker you will encounter many players who, after each session, go home and write down everything they've seen at the table. . . . There are players with enormous written notebooks on the habits of hundreds of other players."[5]

Then they act decisively to exploit this information. They look for games with the right kinds of players, select seats that give them the best position, and adjust their strategy to fit *these* opponents.

---

5. Dan Harrington and Bill Robertie, *Harrington on Hold'em: Expert Strategy for No Limit Tournaments*, vol. 1 (Henderson, NV: Two Plus Two, 2004), 179.

Intermediate-Term Information

Winners go beyond just comparing themselves to their opponents' general skills and styles. They know that conditions can change the way they play. Winners take notes about how various people are affected by factors such as:

- Winning, because some people play better, while others become reckless.
- Losing, because they may either play scared or become overly aggressive.
- Drinking, because it affects people in so many different ways.

Once they know how a factor affects someone's play, they keep track of it by, for example, counting how many chips or drinks that player gets. They want to know how that player is playing *now*.

Winners' Laws

1. Focus on other people, not yourself.

Resist your natural tendency to focus primarily on yourself and continually study your opponents. Instead of thinking that they are just like you, try to understand how they think, feel, and act.

2. Apply the principle of "subjective rationality."

Most people's actions make sense to them, even if they seem crazy or foolish to you. Let's take an extreme example: the Arabs who flew those airplanes into the World Trade Center. By our standards they were utterly crazy. However, since they believed that dying in a Holy War guaranteed going immediately to Paradise, their "holy mission" made sense to them.

All of us encounter less extreme examples every day. Instead of dismissing them as irrational, learn how opponents see the situation and what they want to accomplish. Set aside your ideas about how they *should* think and act, and learn how they *do* think and act. Are they playing to win? Are they only socializing? Are they getting a kick from wild gambling? Are they challenging better players? Are they learning from better players? Answering these questions will help you read their cards, predict their actions, manipulate them, and take their money.

3. Objectively assess your opponents *every* time you play.

Consider both their skills and their styles, and relate that information to your own strengths and weaknesses. You can't pick the right games or adjust effectively if you don't know how everyone plays.

Look for signs that anyone is playing differently from their usual way. For example, a strong player on tilt may be easy to beat. Or someone may have gotten coaching and dramatically improved his game. You need to know how everyone is playing *now*.

4. Relate to people on *their* terms.

Go beyond just understanding how people think, feel, and act. Adjust your strategy so that you get and exploit the maximum edge, but preserve the relaxed atmosphere and keep the weak players in the game.

For example, you may learn something by demanding to see cards that a weak player has shown to a third player. If he would be offended, don't do it. The information you gain is not worth the irritation you may cause.

How Do You Rate?

This rating scale assesses your ability to focus on other people.

Circle the number that best describes your agreement with this statement: *While playing poker, I focus on other people, not myself.* (7) Agree strongly, (6) Agree, (5) Agree somewhat, (4) Neutral, (3) Disagree somewhat, (2) Disagree, (1) Disagree strongly.

Circle that number in the appropriate place on page 262.

The Critical Questions

Review this chapter, especially the Winners' Laws and How Do You Rate? sections. Then answer two questions:

1. What are the implications of my self-rating?
2. What should I do differently? List *specific actions* you should take to learn more about other players.

Discuss your answers with someone you trust and take good notes.

9. Winners Consider Complexities

If you're looking for the one right way to play certain cards, you'll never find it.

*—***Matt Lessinger**[1]

The preceding chapters presented too many subjects for most people. They want simplistic advice, but you can't be a winner by applying a few simple formulas. You have to consider poker's frustrating complexity.

Unfortunately, you don't have the time or the information-processing capacity to consider everything. You must therefore assess both the information's importance and your own limitations. Which information is most valuable? How much information can you handle effectively?

If you select the wrong information, mistakes are inevitable. If you try to process too much information, you will become confused and indecisive, a prescription for disaster. Balance the need to consider complexity with your own information-processing limitations.

It Depends on the Situation

People often ask winners, "How should I play this hand?" They are usually frustrated by the standard answer: "It depends on the situation." Winners ask about everyone's position, skill, and style; the size of the pot; the depth of the stacks; and many other sub-

---

1. Matt Lessinger, personal e-mail to author, November 19, 2000.

jects. Most people don't want to hear "It depends," and they hate answering questions.

In fact, they usually can't answer them because they have not counted the pot, thought about the other players, and kept track of all the information that experts record automatically. They want to know a few simple rules for playing pocket aces, a full house, or a flush draw, and *there aren't any simple rules.*

As I said earlier, with pocket fives winners may fold, call, or raise pre-flop, depending on the situation. Winners also plan ahead and use "chess type thinking . . . visualizing how future rounds will be played, given various cards that would come and adjusting present strategies accordingly."[2]

They do "what if" contingency planning: "If the next card is a spade, I will . . . " or "If Charlie bets, I will . . . " Since there can be up to nine other players and dozens of different cards, the analysis can get very complicated.

Many people don't believe the experts. They say, in effect, "How can poker be so complicated?" Only five cards play, the best hand wins, and all you can do is fold, check, bet, call, and raise.

Poker's apparent simplicity combines with this rejection of complexity to increase the experts' edge. David Sklansky believed these factors are so important that he discussed them on the first page of *The Theory of Poker*:

> From the expert's point of view, the veneer of simplicity that deludes so many players into thinking they are good is the profitable side of the game's beauty. . . . Losers . . . return to the table again and again, donating their money and blaming their losses on bad luck, not bad play.[3]

2. David Sklansky, "Pros vs. Wannabes, Part II," *Card Player*, February 15, 2002, 44–46.

3. David Sklansky, *The Theory of Poker* (Henderson, NV: Two Plus Two, 1999), p. 1.

Losers may also read a little, hoping to find a few simple rules or formulas that will convert them to winners. "If you do not have a good understanding of poker's complexity, it is easy to fall into what has been called the 'magic formula trap.' "[4] If there were a magic formula, everybody would play the same way, and nobody would have an edge.

Some of the winners' edge comes from avoiding the "magic formula trap," recognizing that poker is complicated and situational and being willing and able to consider complex information.

In addition to considering more variables than most people do, winners adjust their priorities to fit the situation. Sometimes, position is the most important factor. Sometimes, stack sizes are critically important, but they can be almost irrelevant. The number of opponents and their styles and skills are more important in some situations than in others. Winners constantly ask themselves, What do I need to know *now*?

Adjusting to Your Opponents

The amount and kinds of information you need to consider depend on your opponents. You can beat the weakest opponents in small games by just playing straightforward ABC poker. They make so many mistakes that you can essentially play on autopilot.

As the games get bigger and the opponents get tougher, you must consider an ever-increasing number of factors. In the biggest games, where nearly everyone plays well, you must consider factors that most poker books rarely discuss.

4. Mason Malmuth, "What's Not Important," *Poker Essays*, 23.

Most poker books deal with hands in isolation, but we constantly relate this hand to everything that has come before and will come after.

Most books recommend the right way to play these cards in this position on this street against certain kinds of players. That approach works fine *except* against the tough, observant, and deceptive players you'll find in high-stakes games. . . . They would quickly read you accurately, then give you hardly any action on your good hands, and take you off your weak and marginal ones.

Most books also discuss each street separately, and they hardly ever consider the ways that previous hands and previous sessions affect your own and your opponents' decisions. They essentially encourage you to focus too narrowly and to base your decisions on too little information.

We emphatically disagree. We believe *you should not deal with one bet, street, hand, or even session in isolation.* Whatever you do now is affected by the past and will affect the future.[5]

The Importance of Mental Speed

The more information you must process, the more important mental speed becomes. Since you need to process so much information against tough players, mental speed is very important. It is even more important when you play online. In a cardroom, you can take extra time, but online your hand gets folded. If you multi-table, but think slowly, you can't possibly win.

Good preparation can reduce the negative effects of limited mental speed, but faster thinkers will always have a significant

5. Ray Zee and David Fromm, with Alan Schoonmaker, *World Class High-Stakes and Shorthanded Limit Hold'em.* Not yet published.

edge. You must therefore objectively assess how fast you think *compared to these opponents.*

Information Overload

Although you need a lot of information, too much of it can harm you. You can spend so much time processing it that you can't act decisively. To protect you from information overload, evolution designed your body to process only the most important information.

For example, unlike houseflies, you can't see behind you. In addition, only the center of your eye can see colors and details; most of it can see only large shapes and movements. That structure prevents you from being overloaded with information, but if something changes, your focus shifts.

Learn a lesson from Mother Nature. Determine which information you need *now* and make sure you get it.

Winners' Laws

1. Don't oversimplify.

Resist your natural desire for comfortable simplicity, and base your decisions on *all* the important factors. There are often more of them than you expect or want.

2. Understand and work within your information-acquiring and information-processing limitations.

Since you can't consider everything, work within your limitations so that you can act quickly and decisively. Prioritize the information and work on the most important subjects, not the ones that make you most comfortable.

3. Select games that fit your strengths and weaknesses.

If you play against opponents with as much knowledge as you, but greater ability to acquire and process information, you will lose. For example, if you don't remember exposed cards as well as your opponents, you'll do poorly at stud. If you can't deal with all the subjects that top players consider, you can't beat the biggest games. Pick games in which you get an edge from being able to acquire or process more information than your opponents.

Warning: Most people overestimate their memories and thinking abilities. Make sure you're not kidding yourself.

How Do You Rate?

This rating scale is concerned *only* with your focus while making poker decisions.

Circle the number that best describes your agreement with this statement: *When making important poker decisions, I try to consider every important factor, including ones I dislike thinking about.* (7) Agree strongly, (6) Agree, (5) Agree somewhat, (4) Neutral, (3) Disagree somewhat, (2) Disagree, (1) Disagree strongly.

Circle that number in the appropriate place on page 263.

The Critical Questions

Review this chapter, especially the Winners' Laws and How Do You Rate? sections. Then answer two questions:

1. What are the implications of my self-rating?
2. What should I do differently? List *specific actions* you should take to consider complexities more effectively.

Discuss your answers with someone you trust and take good notes.

PART THREE

Winners Control Their Thought Processes

Introduction: Winners Control Their Thought Processes

Winners not only focus on different topics from losers, but they also think about them in fundamentally different ways. Losers respond primarily to their natural urges, especially their desires to be comfortable and to preserve their cherished illusions. Because winners are so intensely competitive, they resist their natural desires and do whatever it takes to maximize their edge.

Winners are brutally realistic. They know that powerful forces cause everyone—including themselves—to deny reality, and they strenuously resist those forces. They fight especially hard against their own egos because egotism can prevent them from admitting mistakes and their own weaknesses.

All the steps discussed in part 3 help them fight their natural tendency to deny reality. But merely taking these steps won't work without a hunger for the truth. They frequently ask themselves, What is really happening? Why is it happening?

Winners think logically instead of trusting intuition. They know that denial and emotions greatly affect intuition, feel, or instincts. They make their premises as explicit as possible and then use logic to draw their conclusions. When you think logically, mistakes are easy to correct. If your basic premise is wrong, you can change it. If your reasoning is faulty, you can retrace your steps, see *exactly* where you went wrong, change your method, and get it right. If you rely on intuition, you may believe nonsense because it *feels* right.

Winners prepare thoroughly for whatever demands they'll encounter. They use a wide variety of tools such as books, DVDs, online forums, coaches, and hand-tracking software to develop their skills. They take care of their health because unhealthy players can't play well for long sessions. They plan for specific events such as playing in a new cardroom or tournament. They carefully select their games and seats. They thoroughly plan the way they will play their hands. They review their play to prepare for future contests with these opponents and to develop themselves. Most people won't do all that *work.* They just sit down, play, and lose their money.

Winners concentrate intensely because distractions will prevent them from acquiring valuable information and processing it well. Losers let other issues or feelings distract them. They may not even want to concentrate and dislike people who do. They want winners to "lighten up," but winners won't do it. It would reduce the winners' edge, which is what they really care about.

Winners probe efficiently because they realize that just listening and observing won't provide enough information. They make probing bets and use hesitation, facial expressions, hand gestures, and so on, to see how opponents react. They ask questions during and after hands. Losers don't bother to probe, and they may resent people who do. Probing seems too serious, but winners don't care about how other people feel. They want information and probe to get it.

Finally, *winners use feedback loops well* to correct their mistakes and adjust to changing conditions. Instead of relying on first impressions and instincts, they constantly seek new information and feed it back into their mental computers. They keep their minds open so that they process that information well. After changing their perception of the hand or opponent, they adjust their strategy.

10. Winners Are Brutally Realistic

Your success at poker depends not on how well you play but on how well you play in relation to your opponents. . . . This presents a significant problem. . . . Almost all players put themselves closer to the front of the pack than they deserve to be.

—Roy Cooke[1]

Roy's last sentence summarizes a critical problem in poker and all other forms of gambling, denial of reality. You can't beat craps, roulette, slot machines, keno, and most other games, but countless people keep playing, hoping to "get lucky" or to find a winning system.

More than half the people in a survey said they gambled "to make money."[2] Many bookstores sell useless books about how to beat those games. Losers believe what they want to believe, not what the mathematics tell them.

Poker is beatable, but as we saw earlier, very few players beat it. They win partly because they are brutally realistic. In fact, if you deny reality too often, you will certainly lose.

Hundreds of times a night you must realistically assess a complicated situation: your own and the other players' cards, what the others will do, the probability that various cards will come, your po-

1. Roy Cooke, "A Great Game?" *Card Player*, May 10, 2002.

2. The survey was conducted in 1995 by The Social Science Research Center at Mississippi State University.

sition, your own and the other players' skills and styles, plus other factors. Winners think realistically because:

- They want to maximize their edge.
- They want to know the truth.
- They aren't afraid of the truth.

These motives help them to overcome most—but certainly not all—the powerful psychological, cultural, and social forces that make all of us deny some realities. *Nobody* is always realistic. *Everybody* clings to some delusions, but winners have the motivation and discipline to accept most realities, even when they are painful.

This chapter can help you reduce the effects of these forces, but you can never completely overcome them. You will always deny some realities, but the more realistic you become, the better results you will get. You must think realistically about:

- Yourself
- Your opponents
- Our game

Realism About Yourself

We all have defense mechanisms to protect our egos from unpleasant truths about ourselves. We deny or distort our mistakes and faults, even when they are obvious to others. Because the forces supporting denial are so powerful, you must constantly strive to overcome them.

If you aren't realistic about your abilities, motivation, discipline, and so on, nothing else matters much. You won't reach your full potential, and you'll frequently make serious errors, including (but not limited to):

- Playing too many hands because you deny the odds or think you can outplay your opponents.
- Chasing and generally playing your hands poorly for the same reason.
- Challenging better players and tough games.
- Continuing to play when your game is off.

No matter how realistic you try to be, you will occasionally make these costly mistakes because:

- Luck's short-term effects let you delude yourself about your abilities. You can take credit for your successes and blame luck, opponents' mistakes, and other factors for your failures.
- You want to think well of yourself. The more your self-esteem depends on poker, the more likely you are to deny reality about yourself.

Both factors caused absurd answers to a question about the WSOP Championship: "If I get heads-up at the final table and am even in chips with a top pro, I believe I have just as good a chance to win as he does." Forty-four percent of the respondents agreed.[3] They might get lucky, but their chances are certainly less than equal.

Tommy Angelo expressed his opinion about overestimating our abilities in more colorful language: "Seventy-five percent of all poker players think they play better than the other seventy-five percent."[4] I certainly agree, and losers are willing to ignore clear evidence to preserve their illusions.

---

3. Nolan Dalla, "Chasing Dreams: Player Goals and Expectations at the World Series of Poker—Poll Results," *Card Player*, July 16, 2004.

4. Tommy Angelo *Elements of Poker,* 68.

For example, hundreds of hometown champions build bankrolls to challenge Las Vegas. They usually go broke, but they try again and again. Many good players don't travel, but they lose by playing in games that are too tough for them. They could win steadily at, say, $10–$20, but insist on playing $20–$40, even though they lose. They go broke, move down, build another bankroll, move up, and go broke again.

The hometown champions who repeatedly go broke and the good players who keep trying to beat better ones may deny reality about both their skills and their motives. They may believe they're trying to increase their profits, but they're partly trying to prove how good they are, and they can't accept the painful truth: they just aren't that good.

Some mediocre players even quit their jobs to become full-time pros. Thanks to the poker boom, they may survive for a few years. When the supply of new "fish" dries up, they won't win enough to survive. They deny the reality that the odds against long-term survival are very high, even for excellent players.

Shortly before the poker boom, our discussion group asked Linda Johnson and Dan Negreanu, "What are an *excellent* middle-limit player's chances of making it as a full-time pro?" One said 50:1, and the other estimated 200:1.

A few fairly good players have told me that they expect to become top players. The odds against it are *astronomical.* Tens of millions of people play poker, but only a few hundred are top players. As a child, you probably fantasized about being a professional athlete, model, or billionaire entrepreneur. As you grew up and encountered unpleasant realities about yourself and the world, you got over those fantasies.

Poker fantasies are harder to resist because it *looks* so easy to become a top player. There are no educational requirements or qualifying exams. You don't have to be extremely tall, muscular, or good-looking. You see top players on television who don't look that different from you, and some of their plays may seem stupid. But they are as superior to us as Michael Jordan was to your favorite college player.

Losers don't admit that their disappointing results are caused by their own weaknesses. They blame bad luck, don't work hard to improve themselves, keep trying to beat superior players, and continue to lose. Some losers continue this pattern for decades, hoping their "luck will change."

Winners can admit their weaknesses and mistakes. Phil Hellmuth has won more WSOP bracelets than any other player, and he is famous for his egotism and emotional outbursts. But he has written several *Card Player* columns about his personal weaknesses, and he has publicly admitted to making *terrible* mistakes. For example, he once misread his hand and "called off all my chips with nothing! Talk about bad plays."[5]

Roy Cooke's *Card Player* columns have reported many mistakes. For example, "I had made an error. I had folded an opportunity for a positive wager. . . . I had cost myself the positive edge of the bet . . . just like tossing it [$90] into the street. Dumb! Dumb! Dumb!"[6]

That's what you have to do. Admit that sometimes you are dumb, dumb, dumb. You can't develop yourself, nor can you make good decisions about game selection and strategy without being brutally realistic about how well you play.

In fact, you *don't* have to be an excellent player to win. If you're realistic about your abilities and carefully select your games, you can be a consistent winner—even with limited skills. Just play in soft games and attack the weaker players.

5. Phil Hellmuth, "Never Give Up, Part II," *Card Player,* February 22, 2003, 22.

6. Roy Cooke, "Whoops!" *Card Player,* May 16, 1997, 21.

Realism About Your Opponents

Many losers underestimate their opponents and insist that they are just lucky. They may regard an occasional bad play as being typical, or just misunderstand how some opponents play. For example, some expert plays look like mistakes to people who don't understand them. You will often hear absurd criticisms of consistent winners: "Joe can't play." "Mary is the world's luckiest idiot." This delusion is the "flip side" of overestimating your own abilities, and it has the same results: you will challenge and lose to superior players, and you will make strategic errors.

All forms of prejudice are destructive because they prevent you from accurately assessing other people. Political correctness is just another form of prejudice, and it has the same destructive results. Denying the evidence about differences between males and females, younger and older players, and so on is as stupid and destructive as seeing nonexistent differences. For example, older people are usually tighter than younger ones. Women are generally less aggressive than men.

Winners consider all the available information, including stereotypes, and they constantly try to determine how *this individual* plays. They may expect an older woman to be weak-tight, but—if they see that she gambles aggressively—they adjust their assessment. They don't let prejudice distort the evidence, even when it surprises them.

More generally, you should accept and adjust to the reality that everyone—including you—is a complex mixture of intelligence and stupidity, greed and generosity, impulsiveness and caution. Realistically assess how *this specific* player thinks and plays, and then adjust to that reality.

Realism About Our Game

Many losers don't really understand poker. They may think they do, but their conception of poker is a confused concoction of genuine insights, denial of reality, and wishful thinking. It's a very complicated, subtle game, but its apparent simplicity lets losers delude themselves about what poker really is.

Countless losers don't accept that poker is based on probabilities, and all successful poker strategies put the odds in your favor. The most common errors, playing too many hands and going too far with them, are caused by denying reality about the odds.

Many losers claim that poker is primarily luck to protect themselves from accepting that they don't play well. They may also say that cards are random, but—in their innermost hearts—they don't really believe it. They waste time and energy trying to control their cards. They slowly squeeze or study their cards, even though the distraction costs them valuable information. They demand new decks, or a different kind of shuffle, or change seats, or won't play with a certain dealer, or use lucky charms. They can't accept that cards are completely random, and that nothing can "change their luck."

Summary

Realism and denial affect virtually every aspect of poker. Your critical tasks are to resist your own desire to deny reality, while understanding and exploiting your opponents' denial.

Winners' Laws

If you follow four simple rules, you will become more realistic and get better results.

1. Admit that *you* overestimate your abilities and other virtues.

We all make this mistake to protect our egos. We want to believe that we are more talented, disciplined, and so on, than we really are. If you were born after about 1965, this natural tendency has been reinforced by the "build self-esteem" movement. It is so powerful that it has even affected some older people.

You've probably gotten grades and praise you didn't deserve and been spared criticism you really needed. You've believed countless white lies about how good you are. You want to believe that you can be or do anything and that there are no limits on your future, but it's nonsense. *Everyone* has limitations, and you must accept and work within them.

2. Admit that *you* have some unrealistic expectations.

Nearly everybody has them, especially poker players. It's so easy to kid yourself about how well you play and how easy it is to win. Beware, because unrealistic expectations can cause crushing disappointments. Set aside your fantasies, evaluate yourself and the competition objectively, and decide what you can *realistically* expect to accomplish.

3. Get objective assessments of yourself.

To overcome your own biases, you need objective information. Fortunately, it's easy to get. Thousands of professionals and organizations can assess you on virtually every quality such as general intelligence, math abilities, logical reasoning, and social sensitivity. You can get fairly objective assessments of your poker abilities from coaches, poker buddies, discussion groups, and online forums.

You won't like some of this feedback, but you can't develop yourself well without it. You must be open minded enough to accept this information, *especially* when you dislike it.

4. Select your games very carefully.

Many authorities insist that your most important decision is game selection, but you may not believe it or think carefully about game selection. You may take any open seat and then wonder why your results are disappointing.

You must learn which kinds of games favor you. For example, you may do poorly in tight games, but well in loose ones. Or you may love wild games, but lose in them.

If you choose games with the right kinds of weaker players, you will win. If you pick games with tougher or the wrong kinds of players, you will lose. It is that brutally simple.

How Do You Rate?

This rating is concerned *only* with realism about poker. Don't consider your political, religious, or social beliefs.

Circle the number that best describes your agreement with this statement: *While playing poker, I am brutally realistic. I work hard to prevent my wishes and biases from distorting my perceptions.* (7) Agree strongly, (6) Agree, (5) Agree somewhat, (4) Neutral, (3) Disagree somewhat, (2) Disagree, (1) Disagree strongly.

Circle that number in the appropriate place on page 263.

The Critical Questions

Review this chapter, especially the Winners' Laws and How Do You Rate? sections. Then answer two questions:

1. What are the implications of my self-rating?
2. What should I do differently? List *specific actions* you should take to think more realistically.

Discuss your answers with someone you trust and take good notes.

11. Winners Think Logically[1]

Superior judgment requires a logical thinking process.
Those ... who base ... decisions on emotion or instinct do
not stand much of a chance.

—**Mason Malmuth**[2]

Most winners emphasize logic. There will always be some intuitive winners, but the number of them keeps getting smaller. The old-timers were forced to rely on intuition because hardly anything had been written about poker mathematics and strategy, and tools such as computer simulations, odds calculators, and hand-tracking software did not exist.

Because you can use so many books, magazines, DVDs, instructional websites, Internet forums, and high-tech analytic tools, you don't need to rely on intuition. Thanks to these tools and multi-tabling, some "young guns" have played more hands, analyzed them more thoroughly, and know more about poker than Johnny Moss, Jack Strauss, and many other immortals.

Definitions

My dictionary defines "intuition" (aka "feel" or "instinct") as "the process of coming to direct knowledge without reasoning or ... rational thought." Many intuitive players don't analyze their thinking

---

1. This chapter borrows from pages 19–60 of my book, *Your Worst Poker Enemy* (NY: Lyle Stuart, 2007).

2. Mason Malmuth, "Why You Lose," *Poker Essays* (Henderson, NV: Two Plus Two, 2004), 39.

because analysis directly conflicts with intuition. They do what feels right and can't explain their feelings.

Doyle Brunson is the best-known and the most successful intuitive player. He has won millions of dollars, has won the WSOP Main Event Championship twice, has nine WSOP bracelets, and is in the Poker Hall of Fame. In *Super System* he wrote:

> Whenever I use the word "feel" . . . I recall what happened. . . . Even though I might not *consciously* do so . . . I recall that this same play came up (or something close to it) and this is what he did or somebody else did. So I get a feeling that he's bluffing or that I can make a play here and get the pot. But, actually my subconscious mind is reasoning it all out.[3]

Of course, he was not *reasoning,* at least not in the sense that my dictionary and most people use that word. He was just relying on his great intuition, and he did not tell his readers how to apply his type of reasoning.

Instead, he urged readers to trust their instincts: "Once you decide what a man's most likely to have—especially in no-limit—you should never change your mind. You'll probably be right the first time, so don't try to second-guess yourself. Have the courage and conviction to trust your instincts."[4]

For most people it is *terrible* advice. Without solid evidence that you have his extraordinary gift, you should not assume that "you'll probably be right the first time." That assumption is based on an even more dangerous one: that you have great intuition. If you in-

---

3. Doyle Brunson's, *Super System: A Course in Power Poker* (NY: Cardoza, 2002), 551. He recommended this style only in the "No Limit Hold'em" chapter. The other chapters were much more logical, including one written by David Sklansky.

4. *Super/System 2,* page 551

correctly make that assumption, you'll almost certainly make extremely serious mistakes. You can improve your intuition slightly, but you can't make huge changes in it. It's much easier to develop your ability to think logically.

Logic is a completely different process. You break decisions into a series of steps. Both the steps and their order are clearly defined and can be easily explained. David Sklansky, the leader of the logical school of poker, wrote: "When I speak of logic, I [mean] the formal type of reasoning that is characterized by frequent use of words 'if . . . then.'"[5]

His books, including those written with Mason Malmuth, Ray Zee, and Ed Miller, are rigorously logical, and they have revolutionized poker. Nearly every serious player—including the intuitive ones—studies them. They break the decision-making process into elements. The premises are extremely explicit. Probabilities may be assigned to each possibility, and they are added to make an overall risk/reward assessment. For example, if you raise, there is an x% chance that you will win the pot immediately, a y% chance that you will get a free card later, and a z% chance that you will catch a winning card. No individual outcome justifies the raise, but since their combination is +EV, you should raise.

These books urge readers to think logically, to make their premises explicit, and to know *why* they make decisions, rather than relying on feelings. Before I worked with Sklansky and Malmuth, an excellent bridge partner made the same point: "As long as you can tell me *why* you made a bid or played a card, I will never get angry because I can correct your thinking. But if you do something just because you feel like it, I'll get mad."

5. David Sklansky, *Getting the Best of It* (Henderson, NV: Two Plus Two, 1997), 67ff.

By making decisions logically, I can improve them. Conversely, when I rely on feelings, I make the same mistakes repeatedly.

Some intuitive players dislike my logical approach. I told my brother, a NASA rocket scientist, that some people had criticized *The Psychology of Poker* because it was "by the numbers."

He burst out laughing. Every scientist knows that scientific research and writing must be by the numbers. If it isn't, no scientist will take it seriously. Nearly every journal article goes by the numbers, covering all the bases in a logical sequence.

Online forums show how logically today's players think. The emphasis is usually on probabilities and logic. If you argued that a certain position just felt right, you'd be ridiculed.

Poker publications show the same shift. Twenty years ago people frequently wrote about intuition, but it is rarely discussed now. "Feel" will always be a factor, but it is becoming less important every day.

Does that historical trend mean that tomorrow's champions will not include intuitive players such as Stu Ungar, Doyle Brunson, and Layne Flack? Of course not. Some top players will always rely on intuition, but they will also use logic, probabilities, computer simulations, and other analytic tools.

But you don't care who wins at the highest levels. You want to know what *you* should do. The answer is quite simple: unless you *KNOW* you have great intuition, learn how to think logically.

Doing so is *not* natural. In fact, hardly anyone thinks logically without being trained, and nobody always does it. It is much more natural to respond to feelings and hunches. Most players act naturally, and it costs them.

Thinking logically relates to virtually everything, such as playing your cards, choosing your games and seats, and deciding whether to quit or keep playing. Logical thinkers make these decisions by keeping and analyzing either written or mental notes.

They ask questions such as the following: What does that bet mean? Do these opponents play better than I do? Is this game's style favorable or unfavorable? How well am I playing? Can I expect to win or lose?

Some of this book may frustrate you because you are not used to thinking logically about situations, other people, and, especially, yourself. The Winners' Laws and How Do You Rate? sections will make your thinking more logical. They can be tiresome and stressful, but they will improve your thinking and results.

Winners' Laws

1. Accept that unless you have great intuition, you *must* rely on logical thinking.

If you have great intuition, take advantage of it. However, even with great intuition, logic is extremely valuable. You will certainly encounter unfamiliar situations that your intuition can't handle. Then there is no substitute for logical thinking.

2. Don't assume that you have great intuition.

You may have much less intuition than you believe. Most people overestimate their abilities, especially vaguely defined qualities like intuition. They remember their brilliant hunches, but forget when they were *sure* they were right, but were utterly wrong.

Instead of assuming that you have great intuition, get an objective appraisal of it. Unless you have convincing evidence, assume you don't have it.

3. Develop your ability to think logically.

Our educational system does *not* usually develop this ability. Students learn how to memorize material so that they can pass multiple-choice exams, but—except in engineering, mathematics, and scientific programs—hardly any attention is paid to developing logical thinking. You must independently develop this ability. See pages 19–58 in *Your Worst Poker Enemy* for specific recommendations.

How Do You Rate?

This rating scale assesses whether you emphasize intuition or logic.

Circle the number that best describes your agreement with this statement: *While playing poker, I always emphasize logic. I never just "trust my instincts."* (7) Agree strongly, (6) Agree, (5) Agree somewhat, (4) Neutral, (3) Disagree somewhat, (2) Disagree, (1) Disagree strongly.

Circle that number in the appropriate place on page 263.

The Critical Questions

Review this chapter, especially the Winners' Laws and How Do You Rate? sections. Then answer two questions:

1. What are the implications of my self-rating?
2. What should I do differently? List *specific actions* you should take to think more logically about poker.

Discuss your answers with someone you trust and take good notes.

12. Winners Prepare Thoroughly

The battle is often won or lost before *it is fought.*
—**Nolan Dalla,** WSOP Media Director[1]

Nolan Dalla's quotation summarizes this chapter's primary principle. Poker is a battle, and poker players and good generals apply essentially the same principles.

First and most important, you *don't* want a fair fight. You want the largest possible edge, and preparation is the easiest way to get it. Colonel Hackworth, one of America's most decorated soldiers, put it this way, "If you find yourself in a fair fight, you didn't plan your mission properly."

Information is the primary poker weapon, and you should acquire it *before* you need it. Many losers don't prepare thoroughly, and some don't prepare at all. They just sit down and play. Playing is fun, but preparation is often tedious and time-consuming *work.*

This chapter is long for two reasons:

- You must take many preparation steps.
- You may not understand the importance of preparation or the number of essential preparation steps.

Many talented players lose or break even because they don't do enough of these ten types of preparation:

1. Developing their knowledge and skills
2. Staying healthy

1. A talk to the Wednesday Poker Discussion Group.

3. Preparing for specific events
4. Selecting the best game
5. Selecting the best seat
6. Preparing at the table before playing
7. Preparing to play each and every hand
8. Preparing for future hands
9. Preparing for future sessions
10. Preparing for their long-term development

Developing Their Knowledge and Skills

Many losers won't invest time and money in this type of preparation because:

- They dislike studying and related work.
- They arrogantly believe that they are so talented that they don't need to work on self-development.
- They argue that Johnny Moss and many other immortals didn't read books and magazines, watch DVDs, or use high-tech training tools.

But they don't have the immortals' gifts, and most training tools did not exist in "the good old days." Books, magazines, and high-tech tools are powerful weapons. We have *Card Player* and other fine magazines, many excellent books, DVDs, videos, training camps, coaches, Internet forums, and discussion groups. Television lets us see great players' cards, watch their moves, and hear the analyses of commentators and players. High-tech tools, such as *Card Player*'s Odds Calculators, *Card Player* Analyst, computer simulations, and hand-tracking software, collect and analyze information in ways the old-timers could not even imagine.

Your opponents are using these training tools, and you can't stay competitive without using them. Fighting poker battles without them is like fighting gunmen with a bow and arrows. In fact, because they have invested the time and money to master so many tools, today's players know *immeasurably* more about poker than Johnny Moss, Sailor Roberts, Jack Straus, and the other immortals.

People romanticize the old-timers in sports, but objective data prove that they were very inferior to today's athletes. We can't objectively compare the poker immortals to today's players, but modern athletes have shattered virtually every record. They run and swim faster, jump higher and longer, and lift heavier weights. If the gold medalists of 1968 competed in the 2008 Olympics without using modern tools, they wouldn't have a chance.

Progress is even greater in mental activities. Today's physics students know more than Isaac Newton, the most influential physicist of all time. A teenager with a computer can solve problems that once baffled everyone.

To stay competitive, you must acquire, study, and use the same tools as your opponents.

Staying Healthy

You may wonder why I am discussing such an apparently irrelevant subject. The answer is quite simple: it is *very* relevant. Your health can mean the difference between winning and losing.

Let's say that you and I have equal abilities, but different lifestyles. You watch your diet, exercise regularly, and get enough sleep, while I eat poorly, don't exercise, and get too little sleep.

When we first start playing, neither one of us has an edge. The longer we play, the larger your edge will become. I will become more tired, less alert, less patient, more irritable, and so on.

Good health is particularly important in large tournaments. If you are fading out, you can quit a cash game, but you must keep playing in a tournament. Countless players have started out well, but had their play deteriorate because they weren't healthy enough to play well for twelve or more hours.

Preparing for Specific Events

Before playing at a new cardroom, learn its rules. Don't play a tournament without preparing for its blinds schedule, payout structure, and type of competition. Otherwise, you may make expensive mistakes.

Some online qualifiers for the WSOP Championship don't prepare *at all*.[2] Despite playing for millions of dollars and immortality, they don't prepare by playing in important live tournaments, and a few even hold their cards so that others can see them.

Discussion groups can help you prepare for tournaments. Several members of our group prepared adjustments for a large freeroll tournament's number of entrants, blinds, and payout structure. Several cashed. They repeated it before various WSOP events, and several cashed.

More than 2,000 years ago, Sun-Tzu's classic book, *The Art of War*, said that good generals use spies and other means to get information about the terrain and the opposing armies and generals. They carefully analyze that information and plan their strategy. The Old Testament made the same point.

Modern generals often conduct war games (simulated battles) to try out various strategies. The opposing army uses the enemy's strategy, and they experiment with diverse strategies, see the results, and make adjustments. The Pentagon uses computers to simulate battles and entire wars.

2. Alan Schoonmaker, "The Lottery Mentality—Part I," *Card Player,* August 13, 2004.

Football teams use live simulations. Before playing the Redskins, the Giants' scouts observe the Redskins' previous games, and the coaches and players watch films and hear scouting reports. The offense practices against a simulated Redskins' defense and vice versa.

Linda Johnson, a WSOP bracelet holder, war-gamed for "Ladies Night," a six-player, one-table televised tournament. Five friends took her opponents' roles. They studied tapes of her opponents' previous tournaments, asked other friends for "scouting reports," analyzed their strategies, styles, strengths, and weaknesses and played the way each one would play. They used the tournament's blinds schedule.

Johnson tried several strategies, and they jointly analyzed each one's effects. Before the tournament started, she knew how she would play against each opponent and when and how to adjust her strategy. Her thorough preparation paid off. She finished second, got very positive television exposure, and could easily have won it.

These anecdotes don't *prove* the value of preparation, but they and the athletic records certainly suggest that preparing well can greatly increase your edge, and that's what poker is all about.

Selecting the Best Game

Countless talented players are losers or breakeven players because they select the wrong games. You can't select the best games without realistic thinking and thorough preparation. Winners realistically assess their own and their opponents' skills and styles and then select games with weaker and right number and kinds of opponents.

They keep careful records that show, for example, that they do well in shorthanded games, but poorly against very aggressive opponents. Then they play *only* in the right kinds of games (unless they want to learn how to play in other types). Most losers don't keep records that show which games favor them, and they may not even think about this issue.

Selecting the best games also requires thorough preparation in the cardroom, but losers won't take the time to do it. They just sit down in any seat in an enjoyable game.

Nolan Dalla told our discussion group how he "works" a cardroom. He walks around, making mental notes, looking for the weakest players and best action. He wants to know where the greatest opportunity to profit is *at this moment*. Then he puts his name on the lists for *all* the good games.

Even after joining a good game, he employs what Tommy Angelo calls game rejection.[3] He keeps his name on other lists, and he may repeatedly change games. His game can become tougher if weak players are replaced by strong ones. Or another game may suddenly improve when a fish sits down or someone goes on tilt. Or his own mistakes or bad luck may create a poor table image. His recommendation is quite simple: look constantly for the most profitable game.[4]

Selecting the Best Seat

Good generals always consider the battlefield. They want the best position, such as the high ground or with the sun in the enemy's eyes. Poker winners apply the same principle by choosing their seats carefully. Ray Zee, a great player, included "Bad seat position" in "Top Ten Reasons You Lose": "Find yourself in a seat with the wrong player on your right or left, and you can assure a trip to

---

3. Tony Angelo, *Elements of Poker* (Privately published, 2007), 20.

4. Chapter 20, "Winners Are Selectively Aggressive" will have much more to say about game and seat selection.

the withdrawal window of your bank. . . . Many times great games are not worth staying in because you cannot move position at the table."[5]

The Psychology of Poker included a question for every type of player: "Where should you sit?" You want passive or predictable players to your left and aggressive or unpredictable ones to your right. Then you don't get many surprises, and you can avoid the tougher players.

Preparing at the Table Before Playing

Don't start playing immediately. You probably want to post your blinds and get started, but don't do it. Instead, observe a few hands. Because you have nothing at risk, you can concentrate on learning about each player and the overall game. Then plan your general strategy and adjustments to individual players. Categorize each player and the overall game on two dimensions:

1. Tight/Loose (how often people see the flop, turn, and river)
2. Passive/Aggressive (how often they check, bet, raise, and reraise)

Combining these dimensions gives us four types of players, and each requires a different strategy:

1. Loose-passive
2. Tight-passive
3. Loose-aggressive
4. Tight-aggressive

5. Ray Zee, "Top Ten Reasons You Lose," *Two Plus Two Internet Magazine.*

Since *The Psychology of Poker* gives detailed instructions about recognizing and adjusting to each type, I won't discuss these adjustments.[6]

Preparing to Play Each and Every Hand

This preparation involves a new dimension, *time pressure.* You have so little time to make decisions—especially when playing online—that you may not consider enough information. Mason Malmuth wrote, "I think the real reason why some players always outperform everyone else has to do with speed of thought. . . . Those who are able to think quickly through all the possibilities will have a significant edge over those who think at more normal speeds.[7]

You can't increase your mental speed, but you can increase your thinking time by preparing thoroughly *beforehand.* This preparation occurs in two phases, before and after seeing your cards.

Before Seeing Your Cards

You may not acquire any information before looking at your cards. Since you need more information, you have a dilemma. Taking the time to get that information may tell observant opponents that your next action is not automatic. They may then read you more accurately. Or you may rush your analysis and make a bad decision. Winners reduce these problems by getting or recalling essential information in advance by asking themselves such as:

- What is my position?
- What is my table image?

6. You should also consider a third dimension: readable-unreadable.

7. Mason Malmuth, "Thinking Fast," *Poker Essays* (Henderson, NV: Two Plus Two, 1991), 101–102.

- Who is in the blinds, and how does each one play?
- What have the players in front of me done?
- Which kinds of players have called or raised?
- What are their stack sizes?
- How large is the pot, and how many players are in it?
- How do the people behind me play?
- Has anyone behind me indicated that he will raise or fold?

Then, after seeing their cards, they can quickly make a good decision about how to play them.

If you doubt the importance of this preparation, just look at other players. Who asks, "How much is it to me?" or "Who raised?" It's usually the losers. The winners already know the answers. If you ask or have to think about these questions, you're obviously not preparing like a winner.

After Seeing Your Cards

Before deciding whether to fold, call, or raise before the flop, winners do what David Sklansky calls "chess-type thinking." They plan how they will play the entire hand. Of course, these plans depend on the board cards, number and type of opponents, and other factors, but they begin thinking of various alternatives *before* making that first decision:

- "If there is a raise behind me, I will . . ."
- "If everyone folds behind me, I will . . ."
- "If the flop is X, and everyone checks, I will . . ."
- "If the flop is Y, and Joe bets, I will . . ."

Chess-type thinking may seem alien to you. You may think it is too hard or even counterproductive to anticipate what will happen and develop plans for various contingencies. Then, when it is your turn to act, you must rush your analysis. You essentially force yourself to make important decisions without thorough analysis.

Planning is so important that *Professional No-limit Hold'em* begins with these words: "Plan your hand. If we had to summarize this book in three words, [they] would be . . . **PLAN YOUR HAND**."[8]

Barry Tanenbaum certainly agrees: "For many players, planning seems to be the furthest thing from their minds. Planning your play is one of the major themes of my new book, *Advanced Limit Hold'em Strategy.* . . . You must make a plan and keep it clearly in your mind so that you know which plays to make and why you are making them."[9]

As these and other books clearly state, you can't plan your hand well without *first* taking the other preparation steps: learning the odds and strategy, gathering information about your opponents, keeping track of your position, and so on. Otherwise, your plans are little more than guesses.

Making and updating plans also require that you continually gather information. For example, even though it is extremely easy to count the pot as it is being built, you may not do it. Then you must either waste precious time counting it or make decisions without knowing your odds.

As Tanenbaum recommends, you should also ask yourself at least eight questions after the flop:

1. Do I have a made hand, a draw, or nothing?
2. Based on the betting, what are my opponents likely to have?

---

8. Matt Flynn, Sunny Mehta, and Ed Miller, *Professional No-Limit Hold'em* (Henderson, NV: Two Plus Two, 2007), 1.

9. Barry Tanenbaum "Planning Your Play," *Card Player,* August 29, 2007.

3. Do I want to build a pot or keep it small?
4. Do I want to keep opponents in or eliminate them?
5. What sorts of hands can I represent?
6. How likely is a bluff?
7. Do I have or can I gain the lead so that opponents have to react to my plays?
8. Should my approach be active or passive?[10]

Use the time you would have to spend counting the pot, trying to determine which kind of players you face, and so on, to answer these (and other) questions. For example, you should analyze the *meaning* of other players' actions and anticipate how they will react to your decisions. Then, when making key decisions, you will have enough information. Instead of guessing or acting impulsively, you will know *why* you should fold, call, or raise.

Preparing for Future Hands

When you're in a pot, you naturally focus on how to play that hand, but you should also make mental notes for future hands.[11] There are two other times to prepare for future hands:

1. After you fold
2. After the hand is over

After You Fold

Many writers have urged you to study the action after folding. Unfortunately, you may pay little attention to the action because

10. *Advanced Limit Hold'em Strategy: Techniques for Beating Tough Games,* 34.

11. See "Taking Notes" on pages 50–65 in *Your Best Poker Friend* (NY: Lyle Stuart, 2007).

you're thinking about bad beats, lucky catches, the amount you have won or lost, or even what you want to drink. You may even ignore the action and chat or watch television.

Stay focused on your opponents because you can learn more after folding than while playing. When risking your money, you naturally focus on your cards and strategy. After folding, you can see your opponents more clearly and think about them more thoroughly and objectively.

Forget about the cards you folded and the money you would have won or lost. Instead study your opponents. Don't think, "I should have called that raise with my ten-nine offsuit. I would have flopped the nut straight, and look at that action! I would have won a huge pot."

If you watch the action like a television show, you will read your opponents *much* better than you do while playing. You will pick up more tells, see betting patterns more clearly, and get a sharper understanding of the way they think, feel, and play.

After the Hand Is Over

You naturally think more about the next hand than the last one, especially if you weren't involved in it. This is a great time to learn how your opponents think. You probably think that a hold'em hand has only five streets, but Tommy Angelo's book, *Elements of Poker,* goes one street further:

> Sixth street starts when the betting stops. . . . Players relax, which is why it pays not to.
>
> While playing . . . players are stoic, doing their best to give up as little information as possible. . . . As soon as the betting stops . . . they start broadcasting information about their thoughts, their feelings, and their cards. Sixth street is when players let their

guard down, as if all of a sudden it's safe to reveal classified secrets to the enemy. It's like they don't even know the war is still
going on.[12]

You must recognize that—since the information battle *never*
stops—you must *never* give away information. I wrote about this
mistake in "We need a Miranda Warning."

> Every poker room should have a sign saying: 'Warning, anything
> you say can be used against you.' ... *Every time you give away infor-*
> *mation, you are essentially giving away chips.*
>
> "Yet people do it all the time. They tell bad beat stories, show
> their hands, discuss their strategy, criticize and lecture other play-
> ers, and give away lots of other information ...
>
> "The next time you're tempted to talk, show your cards, or give
> away any other information remember the Miranda Warning: *Any-*
> *thing you say can be used against you ...*[13]

But don't keep completely silent. You know that the information
war never ends, but you don't want your opponents to realize it and
clam up. Instead, talk in a friendly way that yields information, but
also preserves the relaxed, "let's have fun" atmosphere.

Preparing for Future Sessions

Winners *never* stop preparing. After a session is over, they prepare for future ones. I asked Barry Tanenbaum, "What do you do
after you finish playing?" He said that he reviews his session to:

---

12. *Your Worst Poker Enemy,* pp. 177–179.

13. Chapter 14, of this book. "Winners Probe Effectively," will suggest ways to information on sixth street.

- Prepare to play against the same opponents.
- Develop his own skills (which he considers more important).

Preparing to Play Against the Same Opponents

Since you may play against many people, ask, "On whom should I focus?" Consider two factors:

1. How often you will play against an opponent.
2. How he plays.

First, focus on opponents you will often encounter. Since you normally play against the same people in home games, study everybody. In Las Vegas, Atlantic City, and other tourist towns, study the regulars and the tourists you will meet again. Ask *conversationally,* "Where do you live?" or "How long will you be in town?" or "How often do you come here?"

Second, focus primarily on opponents who play particularly well, poorly, or unpredictably. Pay less attention to average players since they don't require large adjustments. Study each "target" to learn the following:

- How well he plays
- Which style he plays
- Any tells or telegraphs
- Anything that changes his play
- Any surprises

How well he plays: Decide whether he is so weak that you should try to get into his game or so strong or tricky (or both) that you should avoid him. Decide where to sit to get the best results.

Which style he plays: Learn how loose, tight, passive, aggressive, tricky, or straightforward he is, plus any specific tendencies such as raising for free cards or "floating" on the flop. Then decide where to sit and how to adjust. *The Psychology of Poker* provides detailed guidelines for sitting and adjusting to each major style, but you should also prepare to react to each opponent's specific tendencies.

Any tells or telegraphs: Make mental or written notes about his signals and their meaning. Mike Caro's *The Book of Tells* and Joe Navarro's *Read 'em and Reap* provide excellent general guidelines, but the meaning of an opponent's *specific* signals is much more valuable.

Let's take an easily seen example. Checking and picking up chips almost always means that an opponent (probably a weak one) hopes to prevent you from betting. However, players vary in how they follow up on that "threat." Joan usually makes a crying call, but Harry usually folds. Value bet against Joan, and bluff Harry.

Anything that changes his play: Almost everyone's play changes under certain conditions, but the conditions and reactions vary enormously. For example, some players loosen up when they are losing heavily, but a few get tighter. Make notes about these reactions. The next time you play, track how much he is winning, losing, or whatever else changes his game, and then adjust your play.

Any surprises: Tanenbaum mentally replays every hand that contains a surprise. For example, if a player he thought was fairly conservative three-bets the river with an eight-high flush, he asks, "Why did he do it?" Either he saw something that indicated his apparently risky three-bet was safe or he was more aggressive than Tanenbaum had thought. This review can teach him about one or both players.

Tanenbaum also notes that a player has developed new moves, such as a check-raise bluff on the turn. If he has not seen that move before, he will add it to the opponent's database.

Developing Your Skills

The most important subject to review is your own play. What did you do right and wrong? Why? How can you build on your strengths and overcome your weaknesses? Since Chapter 24, "How to Become a Winner," focuses on self-development, I won't discuss it any further now.

Final Remarks

Preparing thoroughly is the easiest, most reliable way to improve your results. But some players never prepare well. They may even brag about it in the immature way that students brag about never cracking a book. A few of them do very well because, as David Sklansky put it:

> Many of the superstars are freaks. They have an inborn talent for the game as most champion athletes do.
>
> With proper coaching, practice, and study [most people] can frequently surpass people who have much more talent but don't want to study and practice.[14]

Unfortunately, you probably aren't a freakishly gifted player. To make the most of your limited talents, take all the preparation steps. They can be hard, often tiresome work, *but they pay off.*

Winners' Laws

None of these laws is original, nor do they apply only to poker.

14. David Sklansky, *Poker, Gaming, & LIfe* (Henderson, NV: Two Plus Two, 1997) 25f

1. Accept that preparation is absolutely essential.

It is time-consuming work, but you have hardly any chance to succeed without it. Suppress your natural desire to "wing it," and take all these preparation steps. If you won't take all of them, select the ones you are willing to take *and do them well.*

2. Prepare systematically.

Many losers prepare haphazardly. Ask winners you know how they prepare. Then develop a system that fits your specific needs.

3. Use self-development "tools."

Since your stronger opponents are using them, you can't afford to do without books, articles, DVDs, coaching websites, personal coaches, and technological tools. It takes time to learn how to use some tools, but it's a great investment.

4. Use checklists.

Hardly any poker players use this extremely simple tool. They may even regard checklists as a crutch for the feebleminded. *"I don't need them because I know what I'm doing."* Nonsense! *Everybody* occasionally forgets to perform an essential task. Create or borrow checklists to prepare properly and to ensure that you take *all* the steps you want to take.

Checklists are so important that commercial pilots and operating room teams *are required* to use them. If a pilot doesn't check everything carefully, the engine may stop or the flaps may jam, and he crashes. If someone doesn't make sure that all the supplies are available before an operation begins or doesn't count the sponges and other things that go in and out of patients, they may die. If superbly trained professionals need checklists, so do you.

How Do You Rate?

This rating scale determines how well you prepare to deal with all contingencies.

Circle the number that best describes your agreement with this statement: *I prepare extremely thoroughly for poker. I try to anticipate contingencies and to make plans to deal with all of them.* (7) Agree strongly, (6) Agree, (5) Agree somewhat, (4) Neutral, (3) Disagree somewhat, (2) Disagree, (1) Disagree strongly.

Circle that number in the appropriate place on page 263.

The Critical Questions

Review this chapter, especially the Winners' Laws and How Do You Rate? sections. Then answer two questions:

1. What are the implications of my self-rating?
2. What should I do differently? List *specific actions* you should take to prepare more thoroughly.

Discuss your answers with someone you trust and take good notes.

13. Winners Concentrate Intensely

In an otherwise even contest, the man with the best concentration will almost always win.
> —**Johnny Moss,** member, Poker Hall of Fame[1]

Most winners would agree with Johnny Moss because concentration creates a huge edge. While playing, winners concentrate intensely on the action and ignore distractions. They are so extraordinarily single-minded that they rarely think about anything that won't help them win.

Many losers don't concentrate well. Their minds flit from subject to subject, and they may let other issues or feelings distract their attention. Some losers go further: they think that concentration is undesirable and encourage intense people to "lighten up." They don't understand that *winners don't want to lighten up; they want to win.* If something won't help them get the chips, it simply isn't worth thinking about (at least not while they're playing).

The biggest winners have extreme powers of concentration: They study almost every card, bet, gesture, and word. They know how many chips each opponent has, who is winning and losing, and how they play when they are ahead and behind. They remember not only who made each bet but also *how* it was made.

- Were the chips piled neatly or thrown messily?
- Was the bet made quickly or slowly?

1. Quoted by Jason Misa in "The Ultimate Poker Skill," *Card Player,* November 28, 1997, 73.

- What did he say?
- And how did he say it?

Roy Cooke's *Card Player* columns and books clearly illustrate his intense concentration. He considers far more information than most players, and much of this information comes from continuing to study the action after he folds. Many losers "tune out" after folding, but Roy and other winners stay focused, picking up additional information.

Although all winners concentrate intensely, they focus on different subjects. Intuitive players such as Doyle Brunson and Layne Flack concentrate on psychology. They study opponents' body language, listen to their words, and constantly try to understand, adjust to, and manipulate them.

Logical players such as David Sklansky and Mason Malmuth concentrate on mathematics and betting patterns.

Of course, neither type ignores the other subjects. Since both subjects are important, you should obviously concentrate on both. Mike Caro's and Joe Navarro's books can teach you how to read body language. Books by Sklansky, Malmuth, and others can teach you how to calculate odds and understand opponents' betting patterns. But you must pay close attention to get the information you need to apply any writer's principles.

Winners' intense concentration annoys many losers. They want to relax, tell jokes, flirt with the waitresses, make small talk, and treat poker as a game and social event. They may feel rejected when their small talk is ignored or criticize winners for taking the game too seriously. Because it's just a game to them, they can't understand that it's the center of the winners' world.

Tommy Angelo told our discussion group an amusing story. A babbler kept talking to him, but Angelo said nothing. The babbler got angry, stood up, and said loudly, "I'm talking to *you!*"

Tommy quietly replied, "And I'm listening."

Concentration allows the best players to make amazing plays. They pick up and remember signals others would miss. One of them might explain an amazing call by saying:

> About a year ago he bet with this little twist of his wrist. He was bluffing.
>
> He doesn't usually twist his wrist, but he just did it then, the first time I've seen it in months. So I called him, and, sure enough, he was bluffing again.

You may barely remember who was in last *night's* game, much less how they played a hand or the way they bet their chips a year ago, but some top players remember all these things—and lots more.

You will occasionally find intense concentration in small games. Howard, a successful CPA, plays for very small stakes and stays completely focused on the action. His concentration is a huge asset, but being so obvious about it is a liability. It damages the "let's have fun" atmosphere, makes some opponents play better, and drives away the weakest, most fun-loving players.

Many cardrooms are close to horse-racing and sports-betting areas, which are immense distractions. Some people divide their attention between poker, horses, and sports, and they often lose at all three.

Some losers let waitresses distract them. While involved in a pot, a player got distracted when the waitress brought his coffee without sugar. He turned away from the table, talked to her, got his sugar, and asked: "What's the action?" He then made an idiotic bet that cost him over $100. My private nickname for him is "Gold Dust." I picture him stirring $100 worth of gold dust into his coffee.

There are many other interesting distractions. You may want to hit on an attractive member of the opposite sex or learn about the local economy or football team or get the latest political news. *Don't do it.*

If you really want to hit on somebody or you are more interested in politics or football than poker, leave the table and concentrate on attaining the more attractive goal.

Winners concentrate partly because the pay-off is so immediate and obvious. Picking up a signal that causes the right play can yield hundreds or thousands of dollars *immediately.* Conversely, most winners have learned from bitter experience how much it costs to miss a signal. We have all gotten distracted and made dumb plays.

Winners' Laws

1. Concentrate; give the game *all* your attention.

Shut out distractions and pay close attention to the action and players.

2. Select situations that minimize distractions.

Certain casinos, games, seats, and players are naturally distracting, but reactions vary. For example, loud music and babblers distract most people, but not everybody. Some people can't help watching football games on silent televisions, while others ignore them.

Determine which distractions affect you, and then avoid them. For example, if television distracts you, sit where you can't see it. If certain people annoy or distract you, avoid their games or sit far away from them.

3. Use "tools" to help you concentrate.

A "tool" is anything that helps you concentrate. For example, taking notes about opponents forces you to pay attention to them.[2] Pick the tools that fit your personality and goals. If you won't write notes at the table, make mental notes, step away from the table, and use a dictation machine.[3]

4. Don't feel obliged to "be polite."

You are *not* required to make small talk, nor do you have to answer questions. You certainly do not have to respond immediately to a waitress. If she interrupts the game, *she* is out of line because the game pays for almost everything. Keep your attention where it belongs, on the action.

5. Don't be too obvious.

If you're too obviously intense, the game may get tougher. Some opponents may become more serious, and some lighthearted players may even leave. Do your best to *appear* to be playing for fun, while actually concentrating intensely.

How Do You Rate?

This rating scale assesses your ability to concentrate intensely. Circle the number that best describes your agreement with this statement: *While playing poker, I always concentrate intensely.* (7) Agree strongly, (6) Agree, (5) Agree somewhat, (4) Neutral, (3) Disagree somewhat, (2) Disagree, (1) Disagree strongly.

Circle that number in the appropriate place on page 263.

---

2. See "Taking Notes," pages 50–65 in my book *Your Best Poker Friend.*

3. Dictating machines are so valuable that Gus Hansen, a great player, uses one while playing—even when he is on television.

The Critical Questions

Review this chapter, especially the Winners' Laws and How Do You Rate? sections. Then answer two questions:

1. What are the implications of my self-rating?
2. What should I do differently? List *specific actions* you should take to improve your concentration.

Discuss your answers with someone you trust and take good notes.

14. Winners Probe Efficiently

One of the easiest ways to get information is to ask for it.
—**Barry Tanenbaum**[1]

Even though asking for information is so easy, many losers don't ask questions or probe in other ways. They settle for the information that is freely given to them instead of digging for more.

Since winners want as much information as possible, they probe in many ways. Because probing can give information, they probe *efficiently* so that they get more information than they give away.

A "probe" is any action you take primarily to get information. It can be a bet, raise, hand motion, facial expression, question, statement, and so on. The critical issue is your objective: What are you trying to accomplish?

If you're trying to get information, you're probing. If you're trying to build the pot, thin the field, express your feelings, or accomplish something else, you're not probing. Many actions combine probes with something else. For example, you bet, hoping your opponents will fold, but you're also trying to learn from their reactions. The critical element is your intentions, not your actions.

Some actions look like probes, but aren't. People often say, "I raised to find out where I was." However, after they were reraised, they called every later bet. Since they ignored the information, they weren't really probing.

Sometimes checking or calling provides more information than betting or raising. If you check to see what players behind you do

1. Barry Tanenbaum, *Advanced Limit Hold'em Strategy: Techniques for Beating Tough Games* (West Sussex, UK: D & B Publishing, 2007), 64.

and use their actions to adjust your strategy, checking is at least partly probing.

Let's say you're playing no-limit hold'em, have pocket nines, and limp behind two limpers. The button raises, and four of you see the flop of ace-seven-three with two spades. You check behind the limpers, intending to fold if the button bets, but he checks. The turn is an offsuit eight, and both limpers check.

Since somebody would probably bet with an ace, you make a probing bet of half the pot, and everybody folds. Your bet was small because the button's not making a continuation bet was suspicious. Since you adjusted to everyone's actions, your apparently passive action, checking the flop, was partly a probe. If the button had called your probing bet, your suspicions would have become strong enough to shut you down.[2]

Probing During and After the Hand

Probe during the hand to learn your opponents' cards and after it to learn how they think. Learning their cards may seem more important because you save or win a bet or even a whole pot *immediately*. But learning how they think may help you adjust your play and win much more later.

Probing Techniques

There are many ways to probe, and the more you use them well, the more information you will get. Some techniques are directly contradictory because different situations create varied demands. So learn when and how to use each one.

2. This example was borrowed from Jim Leitner's forthcoming book about puzzles and poker thinking.

Check, Call, Bet, and Raise

These are the standard probes, but most players don't use them well. They bet or raise because they like their hand and check or call because they don't like it. To get more information from betting, and so on, decide in advance which inferences you will make from various reactions, then do whatever will teach you the most.

Barry Tanenbaum suggested an example: you raise with ace-king suited, one player calls, another three-bets and someone four-bets (in the Bellagio that has a five-bet cap). If you cap, you learn nothing. By calling, you learn whether the three-bettor caps. Note that the passive action (calling) provides more information than the aggressive one (capping).

Ask Many Questions

Most players rarely ask questions, but top pros do it frequently: "Did you make a flush?" "Are you bluffing?" "Why didn't you bet the flop?" They don't expect honest answers, but hope to learn from the opponents' reactions.

When I suggested copying them, a friend angrily disagreed, "That's unprofessional! I don't like people who ask questions, and I won't do it!" She reversed the usual pattern. Normally, we *copy* top pros' actions. They are the role models who define "professionalism" (even though a few act outrageously for the television cameras). She unconsciously implied that she was more professional than the top pros.

Nonsense! She is rationalizing her fear of looking "unprofessional." We all rationalize our fears, but we must resist *all* emotionally based reactions and do whatever improves our results. I share her discomfort about asking questions, but recognize that not asking them (politely) is *un*professional and—from a profit-maximizing perspective—"irrational."

You may not ask enough questions because you are afraid of

looking ignorant or offending people. Admitting your ignorance may be embarrassing, but not asking enough questions reduces your information, which will cause mistakes, cost you money, and make you look even more foolish. Fear of offending is natural, but harmful. Never forget that poker is a predatory, power-oriented game, and information is power. If your discomfort prevents you from getting information, you give away both power and chips.

Resist your fears and discomfort, and apply this book's central theme: *The critical difference between winners and losers is that winners do whatever works, while losers do whatever makes them comfortable.*

Ask Both Kinds of Questions

Closed- and open-ended questions provide different kinds of information. Use the type that will produce the right information.

Closed-ended questions (which may look like statements) are generally asked during the hand to get specific information: "Do you have a flush?" or "I put you on ace-king." Most opponents evade them or lie, but their voice or body language may give them away.

Pros often ask closed-ended questions because they can read voices and body language. If you can't read them, do what most pros have done: read Mike Caro's *Book of Tells* and Joe Navarro's *Read 'em and Reap.*

Open-ended questions are usually asked after the hand to learn how opponents think and play. They encourage longer and broader responses by asking for opinions and feelings. The answers or reactions to them help you to understand how people think and play. That information often has greater long-term value than their specific cards.

People are usually more willing to answer open-ended questions than closed-ended ones. They don't want to reveal their cards, but may enjoy talking about their thoughts and feelings. Besides, when the hand is over, they relax and become more willing to talk. So ask open-ended questions about *why* they made certain plays. You may be pleasantly surprised by how much information you get.

Probe Gently

Gentle probes are questions, statements, or actions that relax people and open them up. They create a natural, conversational atmosphere, which reduces both your own and your opponents' discomfort. The critical points are the way you act and how they perceive you.

If you seem interested in understanding them, they are much more likely to respond positively. As Tanenbaum put it, asking questions "is the friendly thing to do, and it's more fun than just sitting there like a puma in the tall weeds, waiting to pounce."[3]

Comment on Specific Plays

If you comment, your opponents may explain why they made certain plays, helping you understand their thinking. Compliments are particularly effective because people love to hear them. They may gladly explain their thinking if you say:

"Great three-bet!"

"Wow, what a brilliant laydown."

"That was an amazing value bet. I couldn't have done it."

Compliments and other comments can provide valuable information about the individual *and* other players. For example, someone may say that he three-bet because the raiser is a Maniac or he folded because the bettor is a Rock.

Compliments that compare a recent move to an individual's pre-

---

3. Barry Tanenbaum, *Advanced Limit Hold'em Strategy* (West Sussex, UK: D & B Publishing, 2007) 64.

vious game can start an extraordinarily revealing conversation. I've had a few conversations that went something like this:

"Bill, I've never seen you semi-bluff with a draw on the turn. Nice play."

"Al, my coach, said I was playing too conservatively. That's just one of the moves he recommended."

"So you've really changed your game?"

"Yeah, I've decided to . . ."

Conversations like that can completely change your conception of how an opponent thinks and plays.

Gentle criticisms can also elicit valuable information, but *never* make the obnoxious criticisms that we hear so often. Here are a few examples from *The Psychology of Poker:*

"I wonder why you didn't check-raise."

"I'm surprised that you called with that hand."

"Why would you try to bluff such a loose player?"

"That was a strange raise."[4]

Gentle criticisms can work because "many people have a strong desire to be understood. . . . For example, [they may] defend calling or raising with bad cards by explaining their reasons.[5]

"Occasionally, someone will object to your probing. So what?"[6] You want to learn how people think, and even their objections may teach you something. For example, if a guy reacts negatively *only* when you mention his lack of aggression, he is probably sensitive about being too passive.

Of course, if you irritate someone, back down. Don't slow the game down or destroy the "let's have fun" atmosphere.

---

4. Alan Schoonmaker, *The Psychology of Poker* (Henderson, NV: Two Plus Two, 2000), 102–103.

5. Ibid.

6. Ibid.

Pause After Probing

Pausing encourages more informative responses. Many people can't handle silence and speak without thinking. If you keep talking, you relieve the "pressure" and give them time to prepare a deceptive answer. An unprepared reaction is probably more honest.

Once they start talking, silence can encourage them to expand their remarks. In fact, the important information often comes last. Many people start by answering questions evasively and then say what really counts.

Don't change the subject or ask additional questions. They may feel cross-examined and become stubborn or evasive. Pausing gives them time to answer, creates the pressure of silence, and communicates your respectful desire to understand them. They may then talk more freely.

Follow Up Your Probes

After you have gotten some information, follow up by probing further or using the information you just got. Since using information will be covered in later chapters, I will discuss only further probing.

You will often get more information just by indicating, verbally or nonverbally, that you don't understand someone. Nearly everyone wants to be understood. If you look confused, that player may believe you're stupid but may also give you valuable information. You can:

- Look baffled.
- Say, "I don't understand."
- Ask another question, "Why did you think he was weak?"

Hesitate and Look Left

You may think that hesitating is not probing, but it can cause opponents to reveal their intentions. Some people are so eager to act or so uninterested in this hand that they indicate what they intend to do. Weak players—especially in smaller games—make extremely obvious signals such as reaching for their chips, picking them up, or starting to fold their cards. A few terrible players even act out of turn.

Better players send less obvious, but still informative, signals. For example, if someone is ignoring the action, he will probably fold. If he is intently studying the action, he will probably call or raise.

Time Your Probes

When you probe can be as important as *how* you probe. Of course, a combination of the right technique and good timing is best.

Closed-ended questions are more effective while you are playing a hand. If an opponent's reactions tell you which cards he holds, you make or save money.

Open-ended questions are much more effective when the hand is over because your opponents relax. As Tommy Angelo put it, "It's like they don't even know the war is still going on."[7] Opponents will often answer questions they would reject while playing. So study the action to prepare your questions, and then ask them in ways that encourage opponents to give away valuable information.

Emotional people are exceptionally careless about giving away information. Let's say someone is happily stacking his chips after winning a huge pot with weak cards. If you ask *respectfully* why he played them, you may learn how he thinks. You may also learn

7. See Tommy Angelo's comments on "sixth street" on page 128.

something useful about other players. For example, he may say that the bettor has a tell that his cards are weak. He may even describe that tell!

Angry people can be equally informative. If someone just lost a big pot, show sympathy by saying, "You sure have been unlucky tonight." He may explain his entire strategy and tell you all about the other players.

The Downsides of Probing

Virtually all probes can give away information, and you may give away more than you get. For example, if you raise "to see where you are," you tell opponents something about your hand. Asking, "Do you have a flush?" suggests that you don't have one, but can beat any other hand. Observant opponents may then read you more accurately.

Some probes give away a great deal of information. For example, at the Final Table of the 1999 Tournament of Champions, Louis Asmo made a huge raise with pocket aces. After going into the tank for a long time, David Chiu folded his kings face up. It was an indirect probe, essentially asking Asmo, "Do you have aces?" Asmo then made the *terrible* mistake of showing his aces.

Chiu's probe worked wonderfully. Instead of wondering if he had made a big mistake, he learned that he had made a great play. It built his confidence and helped him win the tournament. If he had been wondering about whether he had made a mistake, he might not have won it.

But Chiu took a huge risk. He showed Asmo *and everyone else* that he would fold kings for a big bet. That information almost invites people to take shots at him. In addition, if someone had seen a tell, showing his kings confirmed it.

Probing can also help opponents recognize and correct weaknesses. For example, asking, "Why didn't you check-raise?" can cause someone to check-raise more often, and he may then check-raise *you.*

Probing, particularly if it is done tactlessly, can harm the relaxed atmosphere and make opponents play more seriously. Probing gently can reduce this problem, but it is part of the price of getting information. Remember, the battle for information never ends, and all battles have downsides.

However, if opponents "seem genuinely irritated, it is often better to back off since this might affect the mood of the game and even drive a weak player from the table."[8]

In other words, probing is like everything else. The critical question is always whether the benefits exceed the costs. If your probing significantly damages the game or the information you get isn't worth what you're paying for it, back off. If the atmosphere isn't seriously harmed and you're getting better information than you're giving away, keep probing.

Winners' Laws

Because most players don't probe enough, the central theme in these Winners' Laws is extremely simple: *Do it!*

1. Probe frequently.

Because the information battle determines your results, resist your inhibitions and probe whenever and however you can.

---

8. *The Psychology of Poker,* 103.

2. Use many probing methods.

If you use only the most comfortable methods, you will not get important information. Expand your arsenal of probing "weapons" by continually experimenting. Study and copy the good players.

3. Listen when other people probe.

Tommy Angelo doesn't probe, but he listens carefully when others do. So he gives away nothing, while learning about *both* opponents, the one who probes and the one who is being probed.

4. Learn where and when to use various techniques.

This chapter has suggested some guidelines, but you should go much further. Try different ones in various situations. Watch how good players vary their probes. See how people react to diverse probes and try to understand the reasons for their reactions.

It may be difficult and even painful to develop probing skills, especially if you feel inhibited. But you *need* that information, and "getting information is like panning for gold; it takes a lot of work to get a little bit of it. But it's worth the effort."[9]

How Do You Rate?

This rating scale evaluates how well you probe. Circle the number that best describes your agreement with this statement: *I probe exceptionally well; I time probes well and use many probing techniques.* (7) Agree strongly, (6) Agree, (5) Agree somewhat, (4) Neutral, (3) Disagree somewhat, (2) Disagree, (1) Disagree strongly.

Circle that number in the appropriate place on page 264.

9. Ibid.

The Critical Questions

Review this chapter, especially the Winners' Laws and How Do You Rate? sections. Then answer two questions:

1. What are the implications of my self-rating?
2. What should I do differently? List the *specific probing actions* you should take.

Discuss your answers with someone you trust and take good notes.

15. Winners Use Feedback Loops Well

One of the bigger mistakes made in poker is not to reevaluate the situation when you get additional information.

> —**Bob Ciaffone,** professional player and author[1]

Bob Ciaffone is referring to a key difference between winners and losers: winners are much better at using feedback loops. Poker writers rarely use that term, but it is quite common in engineering.

Feedback loops use new information to adjust a system. For example, if the temperature falls a few degrees, a thermostat turns on the heat. After the temperature rises a little, it turns off the heat. These small corrections prevent the room from becoming too hot or too cold.

Poker winners apply feedback loop principles to think more realistically. They accept their own limitations, continuously look for new information, and keep their minds open so that they understand and adjust to it. They know that their hopes, fears, moods, and traits can cause mistakes.

Certain kinds of losers are especially likely to make specific mistakes:

---

1. Bob Ciaffone, "Controversial Hands—Part II," *Card Player,* March 14, 2003, 48. This chapter borrows from "The Feedback Loop," pages 107–132 of my book *Negotiate to Win: Gaining the Psychological Edge* (Englewood Cliffs, NJ: Prentice Hall, 1989). Because I have combined quoted and paraphrased material, I have omitted quotation marks.

- *Loose players are optimists who look for excuses to play.* They hope their opponents' have hands they can beat and ignore contrary evidence. They also underestimate their opponents and overestimate their own abilities.
- *Weak-tight players are pessimists who look for excuses to fold.* They fear that opponents have better hands and ignore contrary evidence. They rarely make deceptive moves because they depend heavily on having the best hand.

Winning and losing change the way many people perceive situations. When they are winning, they become optimistic and expect to keep winning. When they are losing, they become pessimistic and expect to keep losing. Both types of expectations are harmful, but moderate optimism is much better than moderate pessimism. Moderate optimism can make you play more aggressively and decisively, but excessive optimism can cause you to take foolish chances.

Realism is, of course, better than either optimism or pessimism. Because they are so realistic, winners use feedback loops for two reasons:

1. They want to prevent small miscalculations from becoming serious mistakes.
2. They want to adjust to changing situations.

To use feedback loops well you must be brutally realistic and take four steps:

1. *Acquire information continually* by preparing, concentrating, and probing.
2. *Interpret that information.* What does it mean? How does it change your conclusions?

3. *Use that information to revise your strategy.* What should you *do* differently?
4. *Implement that new strategy well.* No matter how good your new strategy is, you gain nothing unless you implement it well.

The relationship between these steps is often circular. While interpreting information, you may recognize that you need more of it. While revising your strategy, you may see that you have misunderstood some of the information. While implementing the new strategy, you may realize that it's wrong and repeat the whole process.

This chapter will deal with only the thinking parts, steps 1–3. Step 4 involves acting decisively, which will be covered in chapter 22, "Winners Adjust Effectively to Changes."

A feedback loop has three important characteristics.

1. *Sensitivity* is the ability to detect small deviations. Smaller is better.
2. *Speed* is the amount of time needed for all four steps. Faster is better.
3. *Reliability* is the frequency of errors. Fewer errors are better.

Feedback loops are part 3's final subject because you can't use them properly without applying the other chapters' principles. You should:

- Be brutally realistic: if denial, prejudices, inability to admit mistakes, or anything else severely distorts your thinking, nothing else matters.
- Think logically so that you can identify where and how your thinking is wrong.

- Prepare thoroughly by deciding which information you need and how you will get it.
- Concentrate and probe to get more information.

Because poker is an incomplete information game and conditions change so rapidly, you can't beat competent players without using feedback loops well. You need them for almost everything you think or do, but I'll discuss only three issues:

1. Reading your opponents' cards
2. Assessing your opponents' strengths, weaknesses, and styles
3. Assessing yourself

Reading Your Opponents' Cards

This skill depends heavily on feedback loops. Really bad players focus on their own cards and ignore information from others. Mediocre players focus primarily on their own cards, decide quickly which cards other people have, and then stick with that impression. When they get conflicting evidence, they ignore or minimize it.

Winners keep getting and using information to improve their reads. David Sklansky clearly formalized this approach:

Do not put undue emphasis on your opinion of your opponent's hand. I know many players who **put someone** on a certain hand and play the rest of the hand assuming he has that hand. This is taking the method of reading hands too far. . . . Instead you must put a player on a few different possible hands with varying degrees of probability for each. . . . Theoretically, what we are using is a process of elimination. . . . As he plays his hand, we can narrow down those hole cards.[2]

Some Intuitive Players Won't Use Feedback Loops

It's not natural to think this way, and some intuitive players won't do it. They "put people on hands," then refuse to change their minds. Doyle Brunson, the most famous intuitive player, put it most forcefully. "Stick to your **first** impression."[3]

As I stated elsewhere, if I had Doyle's "feel," I would do what he does. But I don't, and you probably don't either. Countless poker players overestimate their intuition, and they deny extremely clear evidence to preserve that illusion. They remember their great reads and ignore their mistakes.

I therefore believe that you should disregard Doyle's advice, and follow Sklansky's. Think in terms of a range of hands, and then use additional information to narrow down that range.

An Illustration of Sensitivity and Speed

The value of reliability is easy to see, but it's a bit harder to evaluate sensitivity and speed. Let's look at how speed and sensitivity affect the way an oblivious player, a mediocre one, and an expert read cards. In completely separate situations, all three of them believe they have the best hand on the flop. They all bet. The oblivious player may not recognize he is beaten even after his opponents have raised and reraised. A reasonably competent player may need to be raised only once to suspect he is beaten. An expert may recognize the danger without being raised; the look on an opponent's

2. David Sklansky, *Hold 'em Poker* (Henderson, NV: Two Plus Two, 2000), 49–56. His boldface type.

3. Doyle Brunson, *Doyle Brunson's Super/System,* Vol. 1.

face or the way he handles his chips can tell him enough to adjust his read and strategy.

That's what you should strive for—the ability to acquire and interpret information quickly and accurately and then adjust your perception of the situation.

Assessing Your Opponents' Strengths, Weaknesses, and Styles

Because these assessments are so important, you should try to categorize unknown players quickly but keep your mind open. Start by using cues such as their age, their sex, and the way they dress, talk, and handle chips. If an older woman is quiet and dressed very conservatively and a young boy talks loudly and has a pierced eyebrows, nose ring, green hair, and a psychedelic T-shirt, nearly everyone might label them "timid grandmother" and "crazy kid."

The losers would probably stick to their first impressions, while the winners would use the feedback loop. The losers might let the grandmother bluff them repeatedly, long after the winners realized she was an aggressive bluffer. The losers would gamble with the crazy kid, even after the winners recognized he was extremely solid.

Ray Zee and David Fromm use the term "think dynamically" to describe how high stakes winners use feedback loops:

> Instead of making a judgment and sticking to it, they constantly fine-tune their assessment of their opponents' skills, motives, and thought processes to determine how they are playing *now*. These players pay extremely careful attention to opponents, understanding that they are human beings, not robots.

They recognize the toughest players, but closely watch how they are playing *now* because even the best players play badly at times, especially if they have lost a lot of money recently. Equally important, they think about how the bad players are playing and why they are acting that way.

However, their assessment hardly stops there. After beginning to play, they constantly update their views of everybody, paying close attention to:

- What happens to them (such as bad beats or winning a huge pot).
- How they react to bad and good luck.
- Any other changes in their usual play.[4]

The use of feedback loops does not end when a session is over. Winners often make notes about the way people played and the best strategy to use against them. For example, someone might normally be tight and moderately aggressive but get much wilder when he is losing or drinking heavily. The next time they played, the notetaker would quickly learn how many drinks his opponent has had and whether he was winning or losing. He would then make appropriate adjustments.

Assessing Yourself

The most important feedback loop is about yourself because you *can't* be completely objective about yourself. Nobody, not even the most detached, analytic scientist, is completely objective about himself or his actions.

---

4. Ray Zee and David Fromm, with Alan Schoonmaker, "Thinking About Opponents," in *World Class High Stakes*. Not yet published.

Biases are so common and influential that scientific methods use tight controls to minimize their effects. For example, the FDA won't approve a drug unless it's tested in double-blind studies. Neither the patient nor the researcher knows who received a drug or a placebo.

If they knew, the researchers would be more likely to see improvements in the patients who received the drug. They would not deliberately cheat. They just could not help seeing what they expected to see.

If highly trained scientists can't control the effects of their biases, neither can you. Since you want to believe that you play well, you'll unconsciously deny conflicting evidence. To reduce this problem, winners get and use a lot of feedback. To preserve their illusions, losers avoid, ignore, or minimize feedback. A few steps can reduce this problem, but you can't completely eliminate it.

Keeping Records

To protect themselves against wishful thinking, winners carefully record their results.

> If you could divide all the poker players . . . into those who keep accurate records and those who do not, you would find . . . the record-keeping group would be comprised mainly of winners, and the nonrecord-keeping group would be comprised mainly of losers. . . . Record keeping forces you to acknowledge the truth about your results.[5]

Because losers delude themselves and don't keep accurate records, some professionals have said they win a lot from people who pretend that they're "about even, maybe a little behind." Their

5. Barry Shulman, "Shulman Says," *Card Player,* November 24, 2000.

memories are so selective that they remember and exaggerate their winning sessions, but forget and minimize their more frequent losing ones.

As I noted it earlier, winners also record the conditions. They know how well they did in various kinds of games or conditions such as stud versus hold'em, late at night versus during the day, or full tables versus shorthanded ones.

These records help winners to choose the best games and adjust their strategies. They might see that they do better in full games than in shorthanded ones or that their results deteriorate when they play longer than four hours. That information helps them adjust. They play short sessions at full tables.

Because they don't keep good records, most players don't know how well they do in different situations. They therefore can't choose the best games, times, and other conditions.

Permanent vs. Immediate

Winners constantly ask, "How well am I playing *now*?" Then they quickly adjust their strategy. Occasionally, they will reach a painful conclusion: they may usually be better than their opposition, but they are not playing well *now*. So they stop playing or switch to easier games.

Everybody has slumps. We can see them most easily in sports. Great pitchers suddenly lose their stuff and get pounded. Basketball stars miss shot after shot. When athletes slump, their coaches can bench them.

Unfortunately, in poker nobody can bench you, and you can easily blame bad luck instead of admitting that you're playing badly. Let's contrast two friends with approximately equal skills. One is extremely successful, while the other is often broke.

One flew from Las Vegas to Tunica to play during a tournament in a side game he normally beat. After a few unlucky days, he realized that his play had deteriorated. After making a serious and expensive mistake, he quit and flew home. He hated taking the loss but accepted that he would probably make more mistakes.

My other friend is extremely talented but won't look at himself objectively. His A or B games are good enough to win almost anywhere. Yet he struggles to survive because he can't admit that he is playing badly. When he had a terrible losing streak, his play had clearly deteriorated. I tried to get him to look at himself by asking, "What are you doing wrong?"

He angrily replied, "I've never played more perfectly; I'm at the top of my game." He then told a long, angry, self-pitying story about rotten cards, incompetent dealers, and idiotic players. He was soon broke, trying to borrow a stake. His pattern is extremely common. Countless players say, "I've been running bad," but only a handful say, "I've been playing badly."

Your Motives

Losers often pretend they are acting rationally—i.e., trying to increase their profits—when they are really expressing anger, responding to fears, trying to prove something, or impress other people.

Winners often ask themselves: *Why* did I do that? They know that anger, other emotions, or irrational motives can cause mistakes. If they see that irrational factors are harming their play, they take a break or go home.

Feedback from Other People

Many winners get feedback from one or more sources: Internet forums, discussion groups, personal coaches, and poker buddies. Since pages 23–98 of *Your Best Poker Friend* discussed these sources, I will just say that anyone who does not get and pay careful attention to feedback from other people is very foolish.

Winners' Laws

Because so many people don't use feedback loops well, there are more Winners' Laws than usual. You need more than an intellectual understanding of how they work. You need a fundamentally different attitude toward information.

1. Keep your mind open to new information.

Recognize that you can't completely prevent your biases from influencing you. We all see what we want to see or are afraid of seeing. Once you put someone on a specific hand or decide that he is a certain kind of player, you will naturally ignore or minimize contrary evidence. After deciding that you are better or worse than certain players, you may do the same with information about yourself or them.

Until you have solid evidence, regard all your conclusions as tentative. Keep your mind open to other possibilities and continuously look for new information. You may object that Doyle Brunson, an immortal, disagrees, but you don't have his extraordinary gifts. It would be both arrogant and self-destructive to pretend that you have them.

2. Don't wait until your mistakes are obvious to everyone.

Develop feedback loops to identify and correct small deviations before they become large enough for others to see them.

3. Keep accurate records.

You need good records to reduce the effects of your natural biases and selective memory.

4. Develop all the necessary skills.

You need to master all four steps: acquiring information, interpreting it, using it to revise your plans, and implementing those plans well.

5. Relate to people who will tell you the truth, *especially* when you don't want to hear it.

Have at least one person who'll tell you what you need to hear, *especially* the unpleasant information you don't want to hear. It's been called "tough love," and it can prevent you from making terrible mistakes.

6. Make arrangements to get frequent, searching feedback.

Join discussion groups or online forums or meet regularly with a poker buddy or personal coach. You need *frequent* feedback from someone who impartially looks at you. Coaches are so important that the best players in virtually every professional sport use them. Since Tiger Woods has a coach, why should you think you don't need one? Are you better at poker than he is at golf?

7. Make it easy for others to provide helpful feedback.

The easier you make it, the more feedback you'll get. Unfortunately, most people do exactly the wrong thing. They communicate, directly or indirectly, that they really don't want to hear criticisms.

Communicate that you want honest feedback, not reassurance. Most people are reluctant to be honest because you may become insulted or defensive. You may think that you are just trying to "explain" why you did this or that. Perhaps you're sincere, perhaps not, but explaining or otherwise defending yourself can destroy the whole feedback process. Just listen carefully, and then say "Thanks" for their honesty. You'll learn a lot more.[6]

6. For specific tips see "Getting Helpful Feedback," pages 84–89 in *Your Best Poker Friend* (NY: Lyle Stuart, 2007).

How Do You Rate?

This rating scale assesses how well you use feedback loops to correct mistakes. We will discuss their use for adjusting to changes in chapter 22.

Circle the number that best describes your agreement with this statement: *I am exceptionally good at using feedback loops. I always regard my first conclusion as tentative, actively seek contradictory information, and never reject alternatives just because I "have the courage of my convictions."* (7) Agree strongly, (6) Agree, (5) Agree somewhat, (4) Neutral, (3) Disagree somewhat, (2) Disagree, (1) Disagree strongly.

Circle that number in the appropriate place on page 264.

The Critical Questions

Review this chapter, especially the Winners' Laws and How Do You Rate? sections. Then answer two questions:

1. What are the implications of my self-rating?
2. What should I do differently? List *specific actions* you should take to improve your use of feedback loops.

Discuss your answers with someone you trust and take good notes.

PART FOUR

Winners Control the Information They Transmit

Introduction: Winners Control the Information They Transmit

"Poker is a game of misdirection, manipulation, and lies."
—**Barbara Connors**[1]

Parts 2 and 3 discussed the first half of the Fundamental Theorem of Poker, learning about your opponents. Now we will discuss its second half, deceiving them. Sklansky's theorem dealt only with confusing people about your cards, but we will go further and discuss ways to deceive them about your cards, intentions, playing style, and personality. You should follow three rules:

1. Don't give away information.
2. Be *judiciously* deceptive.
3. Create the *right* image.

This introduction will briefly discuss the first rule. The next two chapters discuss the second and third rules.

Don't Give Away Information

Far too many people give away information that comes back to haunt them. They often don't realize how badly they hurt themselves by talking too much, showing cards, and expressing feelings nonverbally.

Bad beat stories are among the most common and foolish ways of giving away information. Winners rarely tell them, while count-

---

1. "Speaking with Baited Breath," *Poker Player,* February 18, 2008, p. 8.

less losers bore us with them. When you tell a bad beat story, you gain nothing, but you can hurt yourself in one or more of these ways:

- You tell people how you think and play.
- You tell people how another person thinks and plays.
- You appear weak and self-pitying.

You tell people how you think and play. They learn what you did and why you did it. Smart opponents will understand and adjust better to you, which is the last thing you want them to do.

You tell people how another person thinks and plays. The more your opponents know about each other, the better they will play, and you *never* want to help them to play better. For example, if they know that Harry calls with very weak cards, they may overcall behind him with a hand they would normally fold. If you were value-betting with a questionable hand, you could lose a pot you would have won.

You appear weak and self-pitying. You may tell a bad beat story to get sympathy, but poker players—especially winners—aren't sympathetic people. If you doubt me, just think of how you react to other people's bad beat stories. Do you feel sympathetic? Do you tune out? If you do either of these things, you're making a mistake. A winner would listen carefully to gain information about the storyteller and his opponent.

Bad beat stories are not the only or even the most serious way that talking gives away valuable information. Countless losers criticize other people's play or suggest ways to improve it. Doing so can drive them away or cause them to play better. It may also tell other people how to play better and how you think and play. The smart players will use that information against you. *When you're playing, don't criticize or give lessons.*

You should also avoid giving away information nonverbally. A poker face is a huge asset. It prevents others from reading and adjusting to you. Tommy Angelo went further and coined the term, "Mum Poker:" "On the outside, mum poker is the classic poker face, extended to the entire body. . . . On the inside mum poker is no complaining, no blaming, no regretting. . . . Or you could just think of it as sit up and shut up."[2]

Mum poker or any other form of controlling the information you transmit can manipulate your opponents' thoughts and their feelings. Poker writers emphasize thoughts, but feelings can be even more important. For example, if they don't call your bet, they may wonder whether you were bluffing. It can distract them, causing future mistakes. You will often see people make "peace of mind" calls just to relieve that tension. The caller expects to lose, but *has* to know what the bettor was doing.

Some players take pity on opponents and show their cards, which is a very silly mistake. Winners apply a very simple rule: "You've got to pay to see my cards." Winners won't give away valuable information, nor will they relieve emotional tensions. They *want* their opponents to wonder what their cards were.

Not knowing may severely distract them. Instead of focusing on the current hand, they may mentally replay an earlier one, wondering, "Should I have called?"—"Did I make a mistake? "—"Is he outplaying me?"

Showing them can be extremely costly. As I noted earlier, this mistake occurred at the final table of the 1999 Tournament of Champions. Louis Asmo made a huge pre-flop raise with pocket aces. David Chiu went into the tank and finally showed and folded his kings. Louis showed his aces, which greatly relieved David. Instead of wondering whether he had made a big mistake, David

2. *Elements of Poker,* p. 88

learned that he had made a great play. It built his confidence and helped him to win the tournament. If he had been wondering about whether he had made a mistake, he might not have won it.

Showing his cards might have cost Louis a great deal of money. He wanted to be a nice guy, but poker is not that kind of game. Openness is often helpful in personal relationships, but it is suicidal in poker.

Be *Judiciously* Deceptive

Withholding information is essentially passive. The next two chapters discuss *active* deception. Chapter 16, "Winners are Judiciously Deceptive," focuses on short-term deception. If your opponents learn your cards and intentions strategy for a hand, you lose. Conversely, if you can confuse them in the right ways, you gain.

However, your attempts to confuse them can reduce your EV for that hand, and the value of various types of confusion depends upon the situation and your objectives. You must therefore be *judiciously* deceptive, making sure that you are creating the right kind of confusion and that it doesn't cost you more than you gain.

Create the *Right* Image

Chapter 17 considers a longer-term issue, creating an image that confuses your opponents about what kind of player and person you really are. Note the word "right." Don't just confuse them; make sure that your image supports your strategy.

The line between short- and long-term deception is somewhat ambiguous. Playing a hand deceptively can change your image, and the effects of playing hands deceptively depend upon your image. For example, if you bet and raise frequently, your opponents may see you as a Maniac. They will give you action on your good hands, but call your bluffs. If you play very tightly, they may see you as a Rock. Your bluffs will often succeed, but you won't get much action on your good hands.

Even though you can't beat good players without playing deceptively, you must always consider deception's two main costs:

- You usually deceive opponents by playing hands suboptimally. You reduce your EV on this hand, but hope to increase your long-term EV.
- Creating a certain image helps you in some ways, but costs you in others.

Do a cost-benefit analysis. If the costs of deception exceed the benefits, play straightforwardly. Losers don't accurately estimate costs and benefits. They just do what feels natural, which is often exactly the wrong way to go. Gamblers like to ram and jam. Conservative people like to avoid risks. Tricky players like to make fancy moves. They may all do what feels natural, even when they should act differently.

You must not just *act* deceptively. You must also feel comfortable about it. If you feel embarrassed, guilty, or ashamed, some perceptive opponents will see right through you. Others will just sense that something is wrong and react in undesirable ways (such as calling your bluffs).

Of course, you must honor the rules. If you cheat or shoot angles, people won't trust you or play with you. You must understand, accept, and act within the rules, *while protecting your secrets.*

16. Winners Are Judiciously Deceptive

Being devious and deceitful is precisely what one wants to be in a poker game.

—**David Sklansky**[1]

Without deception poker falls apart. If we played with the cards face up, nobody would call your bets with a winner, and you couldn't bluff with a loser.

Unpredictability is closely related to deceptiveness. Varying your play prevents opponents from knowing your cards and predicting what you will do. Otherwise, they will take you off your weak hands and not give you action on your strong ones.

You should also deceive them about your intentions. You may bet to build a pot with a good hand, protect a mediocre one, or bluff with a bad one. You may check, hoping they will check behind you, or trying for a check-raise. If they know your intentions, they can make the best play.

If you are easy to read, poker is the wrong game for you. Unless you play against very weak players, you will certainly lose, and by poker's cruel ethos, you will *deserve* to lose. Because deception is legitimate, your opponents will happily exploit your transparency. Every winner knows that if your scruples or feelings cause you to act openly, while your opponents act deceptively—you will lose.

---

1. David Sklansky, *The Theory of Poker* (Henderson, NV: Two Plus Two, 1999), 129.

When Should You Be Deceptive?

Clueless players are deceptive. Because they don't know what they're doing, they can be very hard to read and predict. Since their deceptiveness is accidental, I won't discuss them. I will focus on the people who are deliberately deceptive or straightforward at the wrong times. They make deceptive moves, even when straightforward play would be more profitable (and vice versa).

David Sklansky's *The Theory of Poker* contained the first systematic cost-benefit analysis of deceptiveness. He stated:

> The more your play gives away what you have, the less likely it is that your opponents will make a mistake. Creating mistakes is, in a sense, the whole object of the game.[2]
>
> ... However, there are situations when deception is costly, and straightforward play is best.[3]

Barry Tanenbaum agrees: "When you play deceptively, you are making a theoretical mistake (at least on this hand)." Since you are making a theoretical mistake, "you must have a very good reason to vary your play.... If you cannot explain a good reason to yourself, you should not make the deceptive play."[4]

Generally, the more you need the best hand to win, the more straightforwardly you should play. Your theoretical mistakes become more costly and yield fewer benefits as the probability of going to showdown increases. Sklansky, Tanenbaum, and others have discussed factors that affect deception's value.

---

2. Sklansky, *Theory of Poker,* 63.

3. Ibid., 70.

4. Barry Tanenbaum, "On Deception and Self-Deception: Part I," *Poker Pages,* pokerpages.com/articles/archives/tanenbaum01.htm.

Your Opponents' Ability

The most important criterion is . . . the ability of your opponents. The tougher they are, the more you must consider playing a hand other than optimally to throw them off. The weaker they are, the more you can get away with optimal play.[5]

Because Tanenbaum's book focused on tough games, it emphasized deception. The first two chapters were "Unpredictability" and "The Illusion of Action," and chapter 1 began with these words:

Top players use two primary weapons to increase profits:

- Forcing their opponents into predictability
- Being unpredictable themselves[6]

The Number of Opponents in the Pot

The more players in the pot, the less you gain by disguising your hand. You cost yourself too much when you do. You won't be able to make everyone fold when you bet with a weak hand, and you cost yourself too much when you don't raise with a strong hand . . . [and] when you let your opponents in cheaply, you increase the chances of being outdrawn.[7]

The Stakes

Deception is *much* less important in small games because the players are weaker and there are more of them in pots. You usually

5. Sklansky, *Theory of Poker,* 65.

6. Barry Tannenbaum, *Advanced Limit Hold'em Strategies: Techniques for Beating Tough Games* (West Sussex, UK: D & B Publishing, 2007) 17.

7. Sklansky, *Theory of Poker,* 67.

need the best hand to win, and when you have it, you will get paid off. In *Winning Low Limit Hold'em,* Lee Jones recommended minimizing deception because:

- So many players contest most pots that somebody either has a hand or "will call you, almost out of curiosity."
- "Deceiving your opponent about what you have requires that your opponent be giving some thought to what you have. Often, your opponent is simply playing *his* cards and hasn't really thought about what *you* have."[8]

The Size of the Pot

As the pot grows larger and larger, it becomes less and less important to disguise your hand because good players are not likely to fold any more than bad players are. Nor will good players try to bluff as much when you show weakness because they too recognize that . . . there is almost no chance you will fold.[9]

Fixed Limit vs. No Limit and Pot Limit

Deception is much more important in no limit and pot limit. Limit poker is mostly about pushing small edges repeatedly, while your no limit and pot limit results depend on a few large pots. If your opponents can't read you, you can bluff or get paid off when it really counts.

Sklansky and Miller call it "swapping mistakes." "The key to no limit hold'em success is not to play perfectly. It is to swap mistakes

---

8. Lee Jones, *Winning Low Limit Hold'em,* 3rd ed. (Pittsburgh, PA: Conjelco, 2005) 66.

9. Sklansky, *Theory of Poker,* 66.

with your opponents. You trade small mistakes to your opponents if they will trade back big ones."[10]

Your Own Motives

Your motives are critically important. If you are playing deceptively for the right reasons, you will probably increase your profits. Deceptive moves for the wrong reasons can be very costly. Losers make them because they are bored, want the kick of tricking people, or love to show off.

Some losers even develop the deadly illness called Fancy Play Syndrome. They make fancy moves that cost them money, and they may even get angry with their opponents for being "too dumb" to react properly to their "brilliant moves."

They would rather make fancy moves than play a boring, straightforward—but more profitable—style. "If you want to do this for your own amusement, fine. Just be aware that you are practicing self-deception. You are convincing yourself that by varying your play, you are gaining money. In reality, you are losing money every time you do it."[11]

How Should You Be Deceptive?

The way to deceive opponents depends on many factors, especially their skills and playing styles. My book *The Psychology of Poker* extensively discusses adjusting to different types of players. Their styles are related to the stakes. As the stakes get bigger, the players become stronger, tighter, and more aggressive, but that re-

10. David Sklansky and Ed Miller, *No Limit Hold'em: Theory and Practice* (Henderson, NV: Two Plus Two, 2006), 178.

11. Barry Tanenbaum, "On Deception and Self-Deception: Part I," *Poker Pages,* pokerpages.com/articles/archives/tanenbaum01.htm.

lationship is far from perfect. You will see tight-aggressive players in small games and loose-passive players in larger ones. You must adjust to the way *these* opponents are playing.

Against Loose-Aggressive Players

Don't try to bluff them. . . . They call with almost anything. But what about advertising? Forget it. You don't need to advertise to loosen them up.

Don't try to steal their blinds or bring-ins. These attempts are even sillier since you can gain so little, but lose so much.

Bet into, raise, or check-raise them for value on the later streets. If you think that you have the best hand, overplay it.

Invite them to bluff. They love to bluff. In fact, many of them get a much bigger kick from bluffing than from winning with the best hand.

Check-raise frequently. A check-raise is much less risky and more profitable than with any other player. . . . The danger that everyone will check behind you is obviously reduced, and the profits are greater because many people would fold if you bet, but call if he bets.

Slow play big hands. They will get much more action than you will, so let them make the pot.[12]

Against Loose-Passive Players

Bet and raise for value with weak or questionable hands. You can bet quite weak hands for value because they will call with even weaker ones.

12. Alan Schoonmaker, *The Psychology of Poker* (Henderson, NV: Two Plus Two, 2000), 119–125.

Don't bluff.... It will probably fail because an LPP [loose-passive player] is going to call you with all but the most hopeless hands.

Don't try to check-raise because they will usually check behind you.

Don't slow play big hands.... People may not bet or raise.... You will lose money on this round and increase the chances of someone's drawing out on you.[13]

Against Tight-Passive Players

Don't check-raise.... They will probably check behind you unless they have you beaten.

Don't slow play big hands. The reasons are the same as those for avoiding a check-raise.

Bluff and semi-bluff frequently, but selectively. They are the easiest people to bluff because they will fold quite good hands.

[But] remember that they would not be in the pot if they did not have at least a playable hand, and they probably have more than that.... They will check hands that most people bet. If you bluff because they checked, you may be shocked to see a good hand.

Steal their blinds or antes.... A TPP [tight-passive player] will hardly ever call. If he does call, he is unlikely to bet on the flop or fourth street because he is afraid of your raise, and you will get . . . chances to draw out and win legitimately.[14]

Against Tight-Aggressive Players

Because most of your tougher opponents are tight-aggressive, you *must* be deceptive. Otherwise, they will read and outplay you.

13. Ibid., 168–183.
14. Ibid., 212–213.

Because other writers have focused on tough games with tight-aggressive players, read their books for specific techniques. My book made just a few general recommendations:

Mix up your game. Being predictable is always a weakness, but it can be deadly with them. They read cards well and push whenever they can. If you don't mix up your game, they will soon learn how to read you, then beat you mercilessly.

Make fewer pure bluffs, but be willing to semi-bluff. It is usually easier to bluff good players than bad ones, but TAP [tight-aggressive players] study players intensely. They read tells well, and they have enough confidence in their skill to call with weak hands. Of course, that is just a general principle. Perhaps *this* TAP can't read you. Try him out a couple of times, and follow the guidelines for bluffing TPP. . . . If your bluffs work, fine. If not, you've been warned.

Don't bet marginal hands for value. . . . A TAP would not be in there without good cards; he may well have you beaten. . . . If he has a better hand, he will probably raise . . . if you have him beaten, he will probably fold. . . . TAP can make plays that cause you to make mistakes.

Check-raise less often. The logic is the same as it was for TPP, but it is even stronger because of the danger of a reraise. Since they are tight, they may check behind you. If they do bet, they may have you beaten. Worse yet, if they bet and you raise, they may reraise. If your hand is worth a bet, bet it.

Don't try to steal their blinds. Since TAP do not overprotect their blinds, your attempts to steal will often succeed. However, when they fail, they can be quite costly, particularly if you are in the small blind (because the big blind has position on you). If he calls, you are one on one with the toughest player; your cards are weak; and he has position on you. That's the last place you want to be.[15]

When and *How* Should You Bluff?

Bluffs are the most visible, memorable, and enjoyable form of deception. Making someone fold a better hand is a much bigger kick than just winning at showdown. Anyone can catch winning cards, but bluffing successfully requires judgment, skill, and *courage.*

To get that kick, many losers bluff at the wrong times and in the wrong ways. Their emotions outweigh their profit motive. Matt Lessinger's *The Book of Bluffs* is the definitive work on bluffing, and some of its principles are identical to the ones in this chapter.

First and most important, "the Risk/Reward Ratio (or RRR) . . . should influence almost all of your decisions." Lessinger recommends that you consider three issues:

1. What does it cost you to [bluff]?
2. How much will you win if the [bluff] succeeds?
3. What are your chances of success?[16]

Issues 1 and 2 are usually easy to calculate, and Lessinger focuses on 3, your chances of success. He tells you:

- *When* to bluff by teaching you how to analyze factors such as your opponents' playing styles, calling patterns, and tells.

15. Ibid., 259–261.

16. Matt Lessinger, *The Book of Bluffs* (NY: Time Warner, 2005), 12–13.

- *How* to bluff with many examples and his "Twelve Bluffing Proverbs."[17]

I will discuss only three proverbs.

7. Indecisiveness leads to failure. . . . You must be strong. Any indecisiveness will work against you.

8. A good bluff tells a story that the victim believes and understands. . . . Let him remain confident in his fold. . . . Confusion leads to curiosity. Curiosity often leads to calls. . . .

11. You can't be afraid of running a failed bluff. Some people avoid bluffing for fear of embarrassment. . . . You have to get over that fear, because if you are going to play optimal poker, you will have plenty of bluffs that fail.

What matters is . . . how much money you make from your successful bluffs compared to how much you lose at your unsuccessful ones.[18]

Your primary question about bluffing should be the same as about everything else: What effects will it have on your profits? In other words, *bluff for profits, not for fun.*

Winners' Laws

Being judiciously deceptive is a major difference between winners and losers, but many losers won't believe it. They either play too straightforwardly or make fancy plays for the hell of it. Either extreme hurts their bottom line. Since so many people feel uncom-

17. Some proverbs also relate to timing your bluffs.

18. Lessinger, *Book of Bluffs*, 4–7.

fortable about deceiving others, these Winners' Laws emphasize the way you think and feel about being deceptive.

1. Accept that deception is both legitimate and essential.

You cannot win against even moderately competent players until you accept this reality. If you feel inhibited about playing deceptively, you will lose to anyone who knows how to play.

2. Analyze your own motives constantly.

Repeatedly ask yourself, *Why* am I acting deceptively or straightforwardly? If you are doing it for fun or because of inhibitions, you are probably costing yourself chips.

3. Play deceptively or straightforwardly *only* when it increases your long-term profits.

Disregard your guilt about being "dishonest," your fear of looking foolish, and the kick you get from fancy moves. Do whatever will improve your *long-term* profits. Since you may have to sacrifice short-term profits, make sure that they are worth it.

How Do You Rate?

This rating scale evaluates your motives for acting deceptively. Are you playing straightforwardly or deceptively for rational or irrational reasons? Circle the number that best describes your agreement with this statement: *Winning is so important to me that I always base my choice between straightforward and deceptive play on the effects on my long-term profits.* (7) Agree strongly, (6) Agree, (5) Agree somewhat, (4) Neutral, (3) Disagree somewhat, (2) Disagree, (1) Disagree strongly.

Circle that number in the appropriate place on page 264.

The Critical Questions

Review this chapter, especially the Winners' Laws and How Do You Rate? sections. Then answer two questions:

1. What are the implications of my self-rating?
2. What should I do differently? List *specific actions* you should take:

   - To become more deceptive.
   - To improve your decisions about when to be deceptive and straightforward.

Discuss your answers with someone you trust and take good notes.

17. Winners Create the Right Images

Take [your] image ... manipulate it as best you can, and work with it to get the results that you want. It's not about winning respect. It's about winning chips.

—**Roy Cooke**[1]

Losers present the image that makes them feel good, while winners manipulate their images to increase their edge. They want opponents to misjudge their playing styles, their strategies, and their basic personality. The costs and benefits of confusing opponents depend primarily on two factors:

- *Your strategy.* Trade-offs are unavoidable, and you must make ones that fit your strategy. "The image that helps you to get a lot of action will make it harder to bluff and vice versa. If you don't clearly understand your own objectives and ensure that your image fits them, you may undermine your overall strategy."[2]
- *The amount of time you will play against these opponents.* The longer you'll play against them, the more important deception becomes and the more time you have to amortize the costs of the theoretical mistakes you make to create a false image. If you won't play for long against them, don't invest much in advertising.

1. Roy Cooke, "Perception, Deception, Respect, and Results," *Card Player*, January 23, 1998, 13.

2. Alan Schoonmaker, *Your Best Poker Friend* (NY: Lyle Stuart, 2007), 102.

Types of Images

Winners construct a wide range of images, and a few highly skilled actors vary their image to fit the situation. Winners sacrifice other motives to increase their edge, whereas losers either express themselves honestly or create images that make them feel good. I will discuss only a few useful images.

I'm a Winner

Some winners project an aura of control, confidence, and competence that says, "Of course, I'm going to win. I'm the best player." Some losers look like "natural victims," just waiting to get beaten up. They appear vulnerable, weak, frightened, angry, or confused. They may complain about their cards, the dealer, and the other players. They want sympathy, but get the opposite. Their manner says, "You can easily beat me," which is exactly what opponents do.

The "I'm a winner" image applies one of Mother Nature's principles. Many creatures look strong and frightening to keep away predators. A strong image can make some opponents become weak and hesitant. They may become afraid to bet or raise with their good hands and may even fold winners. The "I'm a loser" image makes opponents think, "Lunch is served," and they enjoy the meal.

Ray Zee and David Fromm, two extremely successful high-stakes players, proposed using a variant of the "I'm a winner" image against strong players. They act very differently against weak ones.

> You must let them know that you're a serious, formidable opponent. Otherwise, they will push you around. In fact, until they know that you're tough, they will test you by taking shots.
>
> They often try to "run over" the newer players. They may just be testing to see whether you will stand up to them. They may also resent you as a possible threat to their livelihood.

Fight back and play a hand more strongly than you usually would, especially by raising on the big bet streets. . . . Most tough players will recognize that:

- You are standing up to them.
- You are willing and able to hit back.
- You are not on short money, timid, or weak-tight.

They would then realize that they can't run over you, isolate you carelessly, and steal from you. They will then avoid you and attack the weaker players.[3]

Barry Tanenbaum, who also writes about tough games, says that top players construct a complicated version of "I'm a winner" image to create fear, uncertainty, and doubt (FUD).

Opponents who are afraid, confused, and disoriented tend to become predictable. They can't make a move against you because they don't know where you are, so they tend to become passive, mostly folding, checking, and calling. They bet and raise only when they have real hands, and they seldom bluff. In short, they become more predictable.

You want to balance fear and uncertainty and doubt. Play tightly enough to inspire fear, but be varied enough to create substantial uncertainty and doubt in your opponents' minds.

Make them understand that you are likely to turn over a good hand, but you might not, so they sometimes have to pay you off.[4]

---

3. Ray Zee and David Fromm with Alan Schoonmaker "In the Cardrooms," in *World Class High-Stakes and Short-handed Limit Hold'em.* Not yet published.

4. Barry Tanenbaum, *Advanced Limit Hold'em Strategies* (West Sussex, UK: D & B Publishing, 2007) 19–21.

Some egotistical losers try to create a winner's image by criticizing other players and lecturing on strategy. They build their egos, but embarrass the weak players, make them reluctant to repeat certain mistakes, or drive them away. They also give away information that opponents use against them.

I'm a Bully

Winning Through Intimidation[5] was a big best-seller, and some poker players use that approach. They intimidate and run over some players by buying many chips, talking and betting aggressively, blowing smoke in people's faces, criticizing opponents, and acting as obnoxious boors.

Bullies get both psychological and financial rewards, but I'll discuss only the financial ones.

They may make others so angry that they play stupidly. This motive is particularly strong in the few nasty people who play well. They want you to become so eager to beat them that you give away your chips. For example, angry people may make foolish raises and calls just to "get even" with a nasty player. . . . players can go on tilt, which is exactly what the nasty person wants.[6]

This image has severe downsides: bullies make the whole game unpleasant, and they often drive away the weakest players. But some bullies have made a lot of money, proving that this image can be used successfully. I dislike it, but won't pretend that it never works.

5. Robert Ringer, *Winning Through Intimidation* (Fawcett Publishing, 1984).

6. Alan Schoonmaker, "Vicious Customers" in *Your Worst Poker Enemy* (NY: Lyle Stuart, 2007), 286f.

I'm a Sucker

A few winners completely trade respect for chips by posing as suckers. They buy lots of chips and act dumb, crazy, or drunk. They fumble with their cards, drop their chips, slur their words, and pretend to be confused: "Whose bet is it?" "What's the bet?" They may have a waiter bring them fake drinks, making them "drunker." They occasionally show cards they played terribly, and they lie about their other hands.

Most winners would not "buy" this act, but some gullible people see a sucker behind a mountain of chips, expect an easy win, but get wiped out by the sucker's "fantastic luck." Some of them keep coming back, convinced that tonight they will beat that "sucker."[7]

I'm a Wild Gambler

Zee and Fromm create this image *only* against weak players.

Gamble with them when the conditions are right. . . . They came to gamble and resent tight players. Don't play foolishly, but you can gamble a bit with them in close situations, even when you have slightly the worst of it. They want action, and you're giving it to them.

If you do all the things we recommend, the weak players will *want* to play with you. They will spend more time in your games than they do with most tough players, and they will give you more action. In fact, if they enjoy playing with you, you will occasionally get invited to join them. They know they are giving away an edge, but it's fun, and they're there for fun. The best thing you can ever

7. Konstantin Othmer, *The Elements of Seven Card Stud* (Cupertino, CA: Strategy One Publishing, 1989–92), 173–178, tell how and why a pro player creates this image.

hear from a live one is, "Come over here and sit down" or "Let's get a big game going."[8]

Please note that Zee and Fromm control this image's costs by gambling *only* when the conditions are right. They give several examples of apparently "crazy gambles" that are only slightly negative EV, such as putting in four or five bets on the flop with good draws and position. Opponents think they are gambling crazily, but they are giving up only a little short-term EV that they expect to get back later.

General Principles

Although winners create a wide variety of images, they generally apply three principles, and a few apply a fourth one:

1. *They create the image that gives them the biggest edge, not the one that makes them most comfortable.* They deliberately sacrifice comfort, respect, and affection for money.
2. *That image is false, but credible.* An incredible image is worthless, but a true image allows people to read you and counter your strategies. Winners balance revealing too much about themselves and acting so out of character that nobody buys their act.
3. *That image is based upon a realistic assessment of themselves and their strategy, opponents, and situation.* They balance the conflicting demands between the ideal image and their own limitations. The most profitable image may

---

8. Zee and Fromm, with Alan Schoonmaker "In the Cardrooms," in *World Class High-Stakes and Short-handed Limit Hold'em*. Not yet published.

not be credible, while the most credible one may not be profitable. The image that helps in certain situations may be counterproductive in others.

4. A few very gifted players (like Zee and Fromm) take a huge additional step: *They vary their image from game to game or even from hour to hour or player to player.* Very few people can do it credibly, and they are very, very dangerous.

Losers' Mistakes

Losers trade chips for respect and comfort. Either they are too honest, or they project an image that makes them feel good, but costs them money.

Many losers project themselves honestly; what you see is what you get. They may be a bit deceptive about their cards, but they don't want to mislead people about themselves. Their need to be honest makes them readable and predictable, which virtually guarantees losing.

A few even tell people their basic strategy and specific inhibitions. You obviously must check to make sure they are not lying, but some people are so open that they can't help themselves. Let's look at a few examples. These statements were confirmed by observations. The comments after "Thanks" tell how winners would use that information against them.

- "I'm not aggressive. I won't raise unless I'm almost certain I've got the winner." *Thanks.* The next time you raise, I'm outta here.
- "I'll always bet the flop if I'm last and nobody has bet." *Thanks.* The next time I've got a great hand and you're last, I can check-raise.

- "If a pot is big enough, I'll call all the way with anything, but I'm not willing to make loose calls for small pots." *Thanks.* Now I know when to bluff you.
- "I never check-raise because I believe in betting my own hands." *Thanks.* The next time you check, I'll *know* you have a weak hand. I can bluff with garbage or bet a marginal hand without fear of a raise.

Vanity causes many players to give themselves away, and some winners exploit their vanity by criticizing them.

"You were lucky to catch that ace on the last card."

"I did not. I had it all the way."[9]

That fool gave away information that could be used against him.

Since poker is a game of deception, players are naturally phony, but winners are smart phonies, while the losers are foolish ones. Winners project a false image to gain an edge, while losers do it for emotional reasons, especially to build their egos. A few phony "high rollers" play in games they can't afford and take stupid chances hoping to be seen as "real gamblers." Some even brag about their stupidity!

"I know the odds are against me, but I like action."

"I knew you had me, but I called that bet because I don't let anybody run over me."

A few men play foolishly to "impress" a woman, but women rarely do it to impress a man. The men may usually play fairly well, but when a pretty woman sits down, they act like stupid teenagers on skateboards, showing off their machismo. "Look at all the crazy chances I'm taking. Aren't you impressed?"[10]

If she plays well, she is impressed, but not the way the show-off

9. These examples are from my book, *The Psychology of Poker* 101–102.

10. Ibid., 143.

hopes. Instead, she thinks, "I'm going to beat the hell out of this idiot."

What's the Best Image?

Like so many other things, it depends on the situation. Consider all the issues and options, and then select a credible image that will produce the best results *in this situation.* "The idea is to match your image to the game you are playing so that you can manipulate your opponents, allowing you to win more money."[11]

Winners' Laws

1. Create the image that gives you the biggest edge in *this* situation, not the one that makes you most comfortable.

Remember the winners who deliberately look like bullies, drunks, or dummies. They sacrifice their ego and comfort to increase their profits. Learn which image gives you the biggest edge; then, create it.

2. Make sure that your image is credible.

If people don't believe it, you'll seem phony and encourage opponents to study you. As Groucho Marx put it: "Sincerity is everything. If you can fake that, you've got it made."

3. Base your image on a realistic assessment of yourself and your situation.

Don't try to project an image that won't be credible. Understand and work within your own and your opponent's strengths and

11. Mason Malmuth, *Poker Essays* (Henderson, NV: Two Plus Two), 168.

weaknesses. For example, some smart players would see right through some of the ploys suggested earlier.

4. *Work* on your image.

After selecting the optimal image, make sure *everything* you do supports it. If some actions conflict with the image you're trying to create, it won't be credible.

How Do You Rate?

This rating scale assesses how well I manipulate my image. Circle the number that best describes your agreement with this statement: *I minimize my other motives and do my best to project the image that gives me the biggest edge.* (7) Agree strongly, (6) Agree, (5) Agree somewhat, (4) Neutral, (3) Disagree somewhat, (2) Disagree, (1) Disagree strongly.

Circle that number in the appropriate place on page 264.

The Critical Questions

Review this chapter, especially the Winners' Laws and How Do You Rate? sections. Then answer two questions:

1. What are the implications of my self-rating?
2. What should I do differently? List *specific actions* you should take to create a more effective image.

Discuss your answers with someone you trust and take good notes.

PART FIVE

Winners Control Their Reactions to Feelings

Introduction: Winners Control Their Reactions to Feelings[1]

Only in love do I see more self-denial, lack of honesty with oneself, and bad decisions based on emotion than at poker.

—**Roy Cooke**[2]

To play winning poker, you need to control your thoughts and actions, and your feelings reduce this control. *All* of us have some destructive reactions to emotions, and denial often increases this destructiveness. To protect our egos, we may rationalize that we aren't emotional or that our feelings don't affect our actions.

We can see emotional reactions and denial more easily in other people than in ourselves. I vividly recall telling a bitterly complaining friend, "Don't get mad at me. I didn't do it." She shouted angrily, *"I'm not mad!"*

Even if they admit that they are emotional, many people insist that their feelings don't affect the way they think and act. Nonsense! We aren't machines. Emotions often affect whatever we think and do. Pretending that they don't is just another form of denial.

You usually cannot make large changes in your feelings, but you can and should control your reactions to them. Winners work hard to control their reactions for two reasons: First, they are naturally controlled people. Second, they know how dangerous emotional re-

---

1. I'd like to thank Preston Oade for his help with this subject. We co-authored two articles titled "Are You Emotionally Ready to Win." *Card Player,* August 1, 2008 (Part I) and August 29, 2007 (Part II).

2. Roy Cooke, *Real Poker: The Cooke Collection* (Las Vegas, NV: Mike Caro University, 1999), 269.

actions can be. Because they place such a high value on thinking and acting well, *winners' thoughts control their reactions to feelings, while losers' feelings greatly affect their thoughts and actions.*

Some losers believe that they should not even try for control. They want to be "real" and to "let it all hang out." Some emotional reactions may be useful in personal relationships, but virtually all of them hurt you at the poker table.

Part 5 is a transition between parts 2–4 and part 6. Parts 2–4 told you how to "Get the Best of It" by controlling the way you acquire, process, and transmit information. Part 6 will tell you how to "Make the Most of It" by acting decisively. When you react emotionally, you harm every one of these tasks. You don't control the way you acquire, process, and transmit information, nor do you act decisively.

If your feelings are strong enough, you may not even care about your results. Your need to express your feelings may become stronger than your desire to win. We have all seen tilted players throw their money away. In extreme nonpoker cases, feelings can become so powerful that they overwhelm everything, even the desire to live or avoid prison. Anger, depression, lust, and other emotions have caused countless suicides and murders.

This introduction will discuss the general effects that emotions have on your poker playing.[3] Chapters 18 and 19 will describe two methods winners use to control their reactions.

---

3. Some of this material was taken from "Destructive Emotions," pages 138–152 of my book, *Your Worst Poker Enemy.* Because I combined quoted and paraphrased material, I omitted quotation marks.

The General Effects of Emotions

Emotions can directly damage your play and make your opponents play better against you. More specifically, they can cause you to make the following errors:

1. *You acquire much less information.* You can be so distracted by your feelings that you miss signals, including quite obvious ones.
2. *You misinterpret the information you do acquire.* You may perceive what you hope or fear, not what is really there.
3. *You give away too much information.* Your need to express your feelings may make you say and do things that tell opponents how to beat you.
4. *You don't act decisively and effectively.* Winning requires cool-headed, decisive actions, but emotions often cause you to act ineffectively. Some emotions (such as fear) make you indecisive. Others (such as anger) cause impulsiveness.
5. *You show your vulnerability, and your opponents exploit it.* Exploiting vulnerability is biologically programmed into our systems. Animals—including humans—automatically attack the weak. For example, if a dog growls, but you stand firm, it normally will not attack. If you run, it will chase and bite you. In fact, even peaceful birds such as chickens will peck a helpless one to death. And children can be extremely cruel to vulnerable playmates.

A Few Destructive Emotions

A wide range of emotions can hurt you while playing poker: unrealistic love for action, fear of risk, aversion to conflict, self-pity, the need to break even, fear of randomness, pride, and anger. Of course, other emotions can also hurt you, I discussed the effects of all the ones on that list in *Your Worst Poker Enemy*.

People vary in the situations that cause emotional reactions, the types of emotions that affect them, the amount of emotion required to cause a reaction, and the way they react. Some players rarely react angrily, but can't control their love for action. Others are usually timid, but take foolish chances when they're losing heavily. You *must* learn where you're vulnerable and take steps to reduce that vulnerability. Otherwise, if the wrong situation arises, you can lose your entire bankroll. Many people believed they would never get so emotional that they would act foolishly, but got hit with a situation they couldn't handle and lost everything.

The Effects of Television

You may wonder how I can say that winners control their emotions when you see some of the world's greatest players acting wildly, even childishly, on television. The answer is quite simple: they are rewarded for acting that way.

Because the television directors want "exciting" shows, they pressure the players to get away from their typical poker-faced, highly controlled solemnity. The directors want outbursts, trash-talking, clenched fists, high fives, screaming, and all the other nonsense you have seen so often. Since they will get more television time if they act wildly, some immature people essentially "play to the cameras." Nearly all winners sneer at the histrionics. You'll see less emotionalism in months of play in the biggest cash game you'll see on a one-hour television show.

How Winners Control Their Reactions

Winners' realism and discipline are the foundation of their emotional control. Instead of denying their emotions, they monitor their feelings, understand the dangers, and do their best to minimize both their feelings and their reactions to them.

They know that the first step is ensuring that they don't get too emotional. Once strong feelings are aroused, nearly everyone acts foolishly. So they avoid situations that arouse strong, destructive feelings.

If they think they are "losing it," they take a break or go home.

Since I discussed these control methods in *Your Worst Poker Enemy*, the next two chapters will focus on two other steps winners take to reduce emotions and control destructive reactions to it.

1. *They accept poker as it is,* not as they would like it to be.
2. *They depersonalize conflict.* They don't take bad beats or superior play personally, nor do they try for revenge.

18. Winners Accept Poker As It Is

You will rarely hear . . . whining from the really good professional poker players . . . even when they are in the midst of a horrible losing streak.
— **Lou Krieger** and **Arthur Reber**[1]

Winners don't whine because they know it costs them chips. They also know that they can't change their cards, the other players, or poker's rules. So they accept poker as it is and concentrate on the only thing they can control: their own decisions.

Many losers don't know or care about the effects of rejecting poker as it is. They whine or blow up for the same reasons they refuse to admit mistakes or to think realistically: they want to delude themselves and escape responsibility. "Most losing players place the blame for their continual losses on external reasons. . . . They make excuses justifying their losses to themselves. . . . It's a hopeless optimism rooted in self-delusion which drags them even further down the losing path. The reasons for their losses lie within."[2]

Accepting or rejecting poker as it is has been a repeated theme. For example, many people minimize poker's predatory, deceitful nature and focus on "nicer" subjects. Others won't accept that cards are random. Others refuse to deal with poker's complexities because they want to oversimplify our game.

---

1. Lou Krieger and Arthur Reber, "What's Luck Got to Do With It? Part 2," *Casino Player Magazine.*

2. Roy Cooke, "A Message for This Year's Losers," in *Real Poker: The Cooke Collection* (Las Vegas, NV: Mike Caro University, 1999), 244.

All these reactions deny your responsibility to deal with poker as it is, full of frustrations and injustice. The best hand and the best player *will often lose*, and you must *accept that reality*.

Don't Tell Bad Beat Stories

Many players bore and irritate us with these stories. The worst beats occur when you lose a pot because someone makes a serious mistake, but catches a miracle card. His foolishness *increased* your EV, but cost you the pot. If you thought rationally about the long term, you wouldn't complain. If bad players didn't make mistakes, you couldn't win, but you may whine about bad beats.

These complaints are often excuses for bad play. Countless losers insist: "I'm a good player, but terribly unlucky." They want sympathy, but get contempt. Winners do *not* feel sorry for them. Since bad beats are inevitable, they regard whiners as poor players and weak characters.

This difference between winners and losers is so important that I discussed it on the very first page of *The Psychology of Poker.*

> Most stories essentially say: "I played my hand well, but this idiot's stupidity and my terrible luck cost me the pot." It's as if a football coach played the films of a losing game, not to learn how to win next time, but to prove they were unlucky to lose.
>
> Poker winners do the same thing as winning football coaches.... They objectively analyze how they and their opponents play, accept responsibility instead of blaming bad luck, [and] work hard on their game.

Winners do not get extremely upset by bad beats. Of course, their first reaction may be annoyance or even anger, but they know that bad beats occur only when the odds favor them, and they *must* ultimately beat players who buck the odds.

Let's look at bad beats' "flip side." For every bad beat there must be a "good beat." If Mary loses because Joe made a mistake and caught miracle cards, Mary has a bad beat, and Joe has a good beat. You would never know it from poker room conversations. You will hear dozens of bad beat stories for every good beat one. Why?

Bad beats provide an excuse for poor results. People can pretend that they are good players with bad luck. But good beat stories say, "I'm lucky." If you're lucky, you don't have any excuses.

Learn How to Lose

Paradoxically, you can't be a long-term winner if you don't know how to lose. You must not get too upset by bad cards, bad beats, losing nights, and long losing streaks. Doyle Brunson and Dan Negreanu, two great players, have publicly admitted that they have been broke several times. Do what they and other winners do: shrug off the losses, focus on your own play, correct your mistakes, and play your best, even when your luck has been terrible.

Scotty Nguyen, a former WSOP Champion, had extremely bad luck during the 2000 World Series of Poker. He lost a critically important pot because a dealer turned over a card too soon. The exposed card was killed, and another one was dealt. The correct card would have won the pot, and its replacement cost Nguyen many thousands of dollars.

Some players would have spent the next day (or longer) on tilt, bitterly criticizing the dealer, thinking about the lost money, and playing badly. Nguyen shrugged his shoulders and played his best the next day. He won that event *because* he accepted his bad luck and focused his attention on the only thing he could control: his own play.

Accept the Rules

Nguyen could have argued that the rule that cost him that pot was unfair, but he knew that fairness was irrelevant. The card was dead, no matter what he said or did. People constantly demand changes in the rules of other competitions,[3] but poker's rules are clear, consistent, and the same for everyone. So most people accept them, and arguments about them are infrequent and brief.

Occasionally, someone complains: "I discarded my hand because he said he had a better one" or "because I could not see the cards." That's tough. The rules say that you must protect your own hand. If you don't, you suffer the consequences, and nobody will have much sympathy.

The same principle applies to any type of handicap. In poker there is nothing like the Equal Employment Opportunities Commission or the Americans with Disabilities Act. There are no ladies' tees, quotas, or special rules to help people who are disabled, older, younger, female, male, a minority, or anything else. You're on your own, and nobody will help you.

If, for example, you demanded an eighth card in seven-card stud because you are disabled or retarded, everyone would laugh at you. I have beaten and been beaten by grandmothers in wheelchairs, smooth-cheeked boys, nearly blind people, obviously retarded or senile players, plus lots of drunks.

Do their weaknesses hurt their play? Of course, they do. Millions of dollars are lost every night by people who can't see the cards. Much more is lost by players who don't understand the game, miscalculate the odds, or can't remember which cards have

---

3. For example, the winner of the America's Cup yacht races may be decided in court months after the race, and there are thousands of lawsuits about local, state, federal, and World Trade Organization rules.

been exposed, but that's tough. If you can't beat the game as it is, don't play poker. If you play and lose, don't expect sympathy.

I'm a Victim

This feeling permeates the schools, workplaces, and courts. If a student fails, he and his parents blame the teachers, the textbook publishers, the government, society, everybody except the student. If a worker performs poorly, it's the bosses' or company's fault. If someone commits a crime, he's an innocent victim of bad parents, bad schools, bad companions, our culture, racism, or some mental disease.

If you are a self-pitying "victim," poker is the wrong game for you. Bad luck and other people's mistakes will often hurt you. Instead of whining, winners regard them as parts of the "beauty of poker."

One of the reasons that poker is so popular is that luck is an equalizer against more talented players in a short period. . . . If the best player or the best hand always won the pot, poker would not exist. . . . Those who . . . make money at poker should be thankful for the beauty of poker, for it is why players keep coming back to play.[4]

Countless players—both good and bad—whine constantly about other people's mistakes even though *every penny of your long-term profit playing poker comes from exploiting your opponents' mistakes and predictable tendencies.*[5]

4. Mike Sexton, "The Beauty of Poker," *Card Player,* November 28, 1997, 16.

5. Ed Miller, David Sklansky, and Mason Malmuth, *Small Stakes Hold'em: Winning Big with Expert Play* (Henderson, NV: Two Plus Two, 2004), 16. The italics were in their book.

Accept People As They Are

Analyze who they are, how they see things, and what they are trying to do, but don't judge them. When I ask friends about other players, they often reply judgmentally: "He's a good player." "He's weak." "He's a doofus."

Those answers tell me more about my friends than about the other players. My friends are judging them rather than trying to understand them. When we think judgmentally, we reduce our ability to understand and manipulate others. Thinking that someone is "weak" or "strong" tells you almost nothing about how you should play against him. If you try to understand his skills, style, and way of thinking, it is much easier to adjust your strategy.

Vicious and Virtuous Cycles

Losers have a *vicious* cycle. Whining, blaming bad luck, thinking judgmentally, and rejecting responsibility, harm their play and results, which upsets them, further damaging their results, which increases whining and so on.

Winners have a *virtuous* cycle. They *accept the game and people as they are and their acceptance increases their edge.* They essentially say, "I accept the responsibility to cope with reality, just as it is. If I play well and select my games carefully, I will win, perhaps not tonight or even this week, but ultimately I will certainly win."

A Personal Confession

I've got to tell a little story on myself. I thought I was really good at accepting poker as it is. I shrug off bad beats, losing streaks, and so on. When Tommy Angelo and I were discussing accepting the game as it is, I suddenly realized that I overreacted to slow players.

I was shocked. One of my greatest strengths is game selection. I avoid tough players and look for weak ones, especially tourists and drunks. *But* I ignored the fact that these people inevitably slow down the games.

I was essentially mimicking the people who got upset by bad beats. They wanted bad players to make mistakes, but never sucked out on them. I chose to play against very bad players, but didn't want them to do what they naturally did: talk too much, drink too much, and slow down the game.

Obviously, my reaction was irrational and destructive. If I chose to play against weak players, I should accept slow games. If I couldn't accept that slowness, I should play against better players.

I hope you learn from my confession. Nearly everyone overreacts to something, and the reaction is much more important than its cause. Every game is a package deal, and you have to make trade-offs, accepting the negatives to get the positives. Loose games are profitable, but frustrating suckouts are inevitable. Tight games are boring, but you can easily bluff. Tough games can be costly, but they can be stimulating and help you develop your skills. Whichever game you play, you have to accept it just like it is. If you react emotionally to *anything*, it will cost you money.

Winners' Laws

Since my only purpose is to help you win, I will not even consider whether poker is fair or unfair. I want to help you beat our admittedly imperfect game, *just as it is.*

1. Accept that the "rules" are essentially fixed.

By rules I mean *everything* about the game, not just the formal rules. Since you can't change anything, any emotional reaction will cost you chips. If you can't accept poker as it is, don't play. If you can't accept a specific game, change games.

2. Accept that luck has enormous short-term effects, but trivial long-term ones.

Poker is *gambling,* and luck plays a huge role in it. If you can't accept that fact, play chess, but don't expect to make money at it. Since a significantly better player will nearly always win, hardly anyone bets on chess matches. Remember, if luck didn't let bad players win occasionally, they would stop donating. What would you do then?

3. Don't make excuses; accept responsibility for your results.

Players do not care *why* you lost or screwed up, nor do they pay much attention to your alibis. They usually feel contempt for victims, not sympathy. If you make excuses, complain about bad luck and other players, see yourself as a victim, and avoid responsibility, you will undermine your credibility and make yourself vulnerable. Many opponents—and nearly all winners—will see you as weak and exploit your vulnerability.

How Do You Rate?

This rating scale measures both dimensions: accepting poker as it is and accepting responsibility for your results. They are not the same, but they are closely correlated.

Circle the number that best describes your agreement with this statement: *I accept poker completely as it is, and I accept full responsibility for my results.* (7) Agree strongly, (6) Agree, (5) Agree somewhat, (4) Neutral, (3) Disagree somewhat, (2) Disagree, (1) Disagree strongly.

Circle that number in the appropriate on page 265.

The Critical Question

Review this chapter, especially the Winners' Laws and How Do You Rate? sections. Then answer this question: How can I become more accepting of poker *as it is*?

Discuss your answer with someone you trust and take good notes.

19. Winners Depersonalize Conflicts

I like you, Alan, but at a poker table I take no prisoners.

—**Phil Dolan**[1]

Phil Dolan's comment expresses the winners' attitude: He is going to do whatever he can to beat me, but there is nothing personal about it. He would bluff me, steal my blinds, sandbag me, or do anything else the rules allow. I will do the same to him, but neither of us will take it personally. It is just the way the game is played.

The link to the preceding chapter is obvious. Once you accept your game as it is, its conflicts should become impersonal parts of the game. Taking them personally can cause many of the problems discussed in chapter 18. Now I will expand that discussion.

You will not acquire the right information. You may become so emotional that you will miss obvious signals from *everyone.* For example, you may become so intent on getting revenge on one person that you miss obvious signals from others.

You will not interpret information correctly. You will distort information to make it consistent with your feelings. For example, if you are angry enough, *anything* can be misinterpreted. You may have heard this sort of exchange. "Have a nice day." "Don't tell me what to do!"

---

1. Phil Dolan is a friend, and he made that comment during a game.

You will be impatient and impulsive. Personal conflicts can create so much tension that you can't wait for the right opportunity to act. You can make huge mistakes because you have to do something *now.*

You will give away information that your opponents will use against you. You may make foolish statements that tell opponents how to beat you. Or your body language may give away your cards or intentions.

You will look foolish and vulnerable. Your "enemy" and others may see that you are off balance, and they will exploit it.

You will not act decisively or effectively. Your anger can cause extremely foolish actions. For example, you may overplay your hands or try hopeless bluffs, hoping to punish your "enemy." The Chinese have a very apt proverb, "Before seeking revenge, dig two graves, one for your enemy and one for yourself."

Because they are so profit oriented, winners keep conflicts impersonal. If someone angers them, they do whatever it takes to become cool and detached. If they can't control themselves, they walk away. It's another example of our principle: winners' thoughts control their reactions to feelings.

Winners also depersonalize conflicts because they accept that *poker is based on impersonal conflict.* The objective is to take each other's money, and everyone's money is the same. They want to win as much money as possible, and they don't care who loses it.

They accept that only one player can win each hand, that deceit is just part of the game, and that being bluffed, sandbagged, outdrawn, and outplayed are not personal challenges or insults. They are just parts of the game. When they lose a hand, they calmly move on to the next one.

Losers take conflicts personally, especially when they get unlucky or outplayed. They may blow up and vow to get even. Some very competent players—and many more incompetent ones—curse other players or think that someone is out to get them. A few will even throw cards or chips at people. They may yearn for revenge and take foolish chances to get it, costing themselves much more than they lost from the original "insult."

Some winners exploit this vulnerability by showing they have bluffed, bragging when they have caught a miracle card, or occasionally laughing at the loser. Then they sit back and take advantage of his anger and desire for revenge.

Doyle Brunson put it bluntly: "Treating a bluff emotionally is one of the most common and costly mistakes a player can make. . . . You'll see grown men get bent out of shape after being bluffed out of a pot. They start playing *angry* poker instead of *rational* poker. Often the result is catastrophic."[2]

In some ways a poker room resembles a golf or tennis club. Most people—especially the winners—try hard to beat each other, but socialize, tell stories, drink and eat together, and so on. This socializing eases the tension and encourages weak players to stay.

Personalized conflicts drive away the best "customers." The weak, passive "pigeons" often refuse to play with nasty people or in a tense atmosphere. Because losing control has so many negative effects, many talented, but angry players, are losers, while less talented, but more controlled and pleasant players, are consistent winners.

Depersonalizing conflicts also increases your freedom. It lets

---

2. Doyle Brunson, *According to Doyle* (NY: Lyle Stuart, 1984), 59.

you attack weaker players and use deceptive tactics without feeling guilty or embarrassed. You are not a rotten SOB who wants to hurt someone. It's just the way the game is played.

Winners' Laws

Since keeping cool can mean the difference between winning and losing, apply three Winners' Laws:

1. Keep your conflicts impersonal.
Do everything you can to win, but do not take the battle or your losses personally. They are just natural parts of the game. Remember that taking them personally hurts you more than your opponents.

2. Know exactly where your interests conflict and coincide.
Some interests conflict, while others coincide. We want to take each other's money, but we also want a pleasant, smooth-running game. Depersonalizing conflicts helps you fight hard where your interests conflict, but cooperate on common interests.

3. Use aggressive tactics *only* when they will improve your results, *never* just because you are upset.
Act aggressively *only* when it is in your interest, and never lose control of yourself. Monitor yourself, and constantly ask, Why did I do that? If you see that you're acting emotionally, take a break or go home.

How Do You Rate?

This rating scale measures how personally you take poker con-flicts. It does *not* concern your reaction to other types of conflicts.

Circle the number that best describes your agreement with this statement: *I never take poker conflicts personally or get angry about them.* (7) Agree strongly, (6) Agree, (5) Agree somewhat, (4) Neu-tral, (3) Disagree somewhat, (2) Disagree, (1) Disagree strongly.

Circle that number on the appropriate place on page 265.

The Critical Questions

Review this chapter, especially the Winners' Laws and How Do You Rate? sections. Then answer two questions:

1. What are the implications of my self-rating?
2. What should I do differently? List *specific actions* you should take to depersonalize poker conflicts.

Discuss your answers with someone you trust and take good notes.

PART SIX

Winners Act Decisively

Introduction: Winners Act Decisively

You must ... act decisively. ... [Being indecisive] is akin to standing in the middle of the street because you can't decide whether to go right or left.

—**Barry Tanenbaum**[1]

This group of chapters comes last because you can't act decisively without understanding the costs, benefits, and risks of your alternatives. If you take the steps described in earlier chapters, you will certainly get the best of it. But *to make the most, you must act* decisively.

The ability to get the best of it is fairly independent of the ability to make the most of it. Some losers know what to do, but they won't take the risks of committing themselves.

Chapter 20, "Winners Are Selectively Aggressive," focuses on the central point of acting decisively. Instead of avoiding commitments by playing too many hands passively, winners wait until they have an edge and then *push* hard *to make the most of it.*

That principle applies to all poker games, but it is especially important in no-limit hold'em. On my radio show I asked Sam O'Connor, author of *How to Dominate $1 and $2 No Limit Hold'em,* "What is the best advice you can give our listeners?" he said, "Lose the little ones, but win the big ones."

Chapter 21, "Winners Push When They Are Winning," analyzes

---

1. Barry Tanenbaum, *Advanced Limit Hold'em Strategies* (West Sussex, UK: D & B Publishing, 2007), 72.

the way losing and winning cause people to violate or apply the selective aggression principle.

Losers push at the wrong time. If they get ahead, they "hit and
run." If they get behind, they play on and on, hoping to get even.
Many good players have gone broke because they could not walk
away from a losing session. They turned a relatively minor loss into
a catastrophic one.

Pushing when winning is a form of selective aggression because:

- Winning suggests, but certainly does not prove, that they
  have an edge against these players.
- Winning creates a strong, even a frightening image. If opponents think you are stronger, they will react less aggressively and effectively to your moves, which will increase
  your edge.

Winners exploit both that fear and their edge by pushing
harder.

Chapter 22, "Winners Adjust Effectively to Changes," discusses
the ability to cope with changing situations. This ability is essential
because poker constantly changes. One card can convert a winning
hand to a loser. Position changes every hand in flop games, and it
can change several times in one stud hand. A game's style may shift
completely when a Rock leaves and is replaced by a Maniac.

Longer-term changes are even more dramatic. In just a few
years, seven-card stud—which was once the favorite game—has
nearly disappeared, and the few games you can find are tough because the weaker players are playing hold'em. And the hold'em
games have gotten tougher because, as I said earlier, there are so
many books, DVDs, coaches, hand-tracking programs, and instructional websites.

Adjusting to changes is rarely pleasant. It's more natural and comfortable to continue to act in the same habitual way, but it's a prescription for failure. Winners do everything they can to learn how their situation is shifting and then alter their strategies to whatever the new circumstances require.

Chapter 23, "Winners Pay Their Dues," discusses another unpleasant reality: You're not entitled to win. In fact, if you don't pay your dues, you're probably going to lose.

That harsh position directly contradicts the emphasis in modern American schools and workplaces. Because they have gotten grades, promotions, and other rewards without working for them, some people think they are *entitled* to win at poker. So they don't pay their dues and get exactly what they deserve: failure.

Winners work, study, and sacrifice. It isn't easy to pay all those dues, but I never said that winning was easy. The choice is yours. You can deny reality, pretend that you're entitled to win, and end up disappointed. Or you can accept reality, pay your dues, and become a winner.

The final chapter, "How to Become a Winner," deals with a rarely discussed subject: *Changing yourself.* Most poker writers naively assume that merely telling people how they should play will cause them to play well.

But hardly anyone plays the way the books tell them to play. There are no solid studies of the success rate of poker improvement programs, but *hundreds* of studies of other self-improvement programs are extremely depressing. Hardly anyone sticks to diet, exercise, and other self-improvement programs.

When I make that point to poker writers, they insist that poker is different. Nonsense! Since dieting, exercise, and other self-improvement plans can save their lives, improve their health, or make them more successful at work, it is naive to assume that people place a higher value on their poker chips. And, of course, the authors who claim that poker is different have absolutely no evidence to support their positions.

This final chapter also describes a conservative, step-by-step plan for breaking out of your comfort zone. It will help you to overcome the discomfort and other forces that cause you to act like a loser. You can then make the changes that will make you into a winner.

20. Winners Are Selectively Aggressive

When you have nothing, get out.... When you are beaten,
get out.... When you have the best hand, make your
opponents pay.

—John Scarne[1]

John Scarne's three sentences started me toward becoming a winning player many years ago. Some of his advice is obsolete, but those sentences will always be up to date. They taught me to wait until I had a good hand and then to attack with it. Most opponents played too many hands, calling with almost anything, but rarely raising. They played good hands almost the same as bad ones.

Selective aggression is poker's strategic cornerstone. Instead of wasting their chips by doing a little of this, that, and the other thing, winners wait until they have the best of it and then attack fiercely to make the most of it.

Most players are not selectively aggressive. They don't control their thoughts and feelings well enough to get the best of it, and they lack the decisiveness to make the most of it. They slowly dribble away their chips. Losers don't have enough discipline and decisiveness to take the four steps of selective aggression:

1. Wait for the right cards; then play them aggressively.
2. Attack when you have good position.

---

1. John Scarne, *Scarne's New Complete Guide to Gambling* (NY: Simon and Schuster, 1974) 690. Of course, you must always consider the EV. If you're currently beaten, but calling is +EV, of course, you should call.

3. Select games you can beat.
4. Attack weaker players.

These rules are obviously interrelated. If you select the wrong game or attack the wrong players, it really doesn't matter how well you apply the other rules; the better players will still beat you. We will discuss each rule separately, but you should constantly try to combine all four.

Wait for the Right Cards; Then Play Them Aggressively

Most players do not wait until they have the right cards, nor do they play them aggressively enough. They waste their chips by calling when they have weak hands, and they do not attack hard enough when they have strong ones. Because they respond passively to the other players' initiatives, they slowly lose.

A few players make the opposite error: They are *promiscuously* aggressive. They attack too often with weak or beaten hands. They are called Maniacs, a very apt term. They occasionally get hot and win big, but usually lose quickly and heavily.

For many games, selective aggression is the *only* winning style.[2] It reduces losses on weak hands because you fold them quickly. It protects you against drawouts and increases the profits on your strong hands because you bet and raise when others would just check or call. Both folding and raising are decisive, while checking and calling are often procrastination, ways to avoid acting decisively.

Occasionally, this indecisiveness is extremely obvious. A player will call for $10, be told that someone has already raised, and put in

2. No-limit tournaments may be an exception. Some hyperaggressive players do very well in them because other players are afraid of being busted out of the tournament.

another $10. He believed his hand was not worth raising, and the opponent's raise indicates that his hand is relatively weaker, but he has doubled his bet. Anyone who plays like that—and many people do—will *certainly* lose.

It takes discipline to be selectively aggressive. You came to play, not to sit, but you have to throw away hand after hand. Then, when the right opportunity comes along, you must suppress your fears and merciful instincts and attack ferociously.

The tight-aggressive style is not at all natural:

> Tightness and related qualities such as caution and control are not normally combined with aggressiveness. In fact, you will hardly ever see that combination outside of highly specialized occupations such as fighter pilots and police officers.
>
> Because it is so unnatural, the tight-aggressive playing style rarely occurs without lots of work. . . . To become a tight-aggressive player takes the right personality, lots of study, and extreme discipline.[3]

Attack When You Have Good Position

Because you have more information, the later you act, the stronger you are. We saw earlier that a winner would often fold a pair of fives under the gun before the flop, but occasionally raise with them in late position. Position lets you make a wide variety of aggressive moves on every street. For example, you can:

- Raise on the flop with a draw, then take a free card on the turn.
- Semi-bluff on the turn with a marginal hand, then check behind your opponents on the river.

3. *The Psychology of Poker,* p. 20.

- Value bet the river with weaker hands than you would bet out of position.

The bottom line is that you should be much more aggressive in late position than in earlier positions.

Select Games You Can Beat

Winners play to make money, not to prove anything. "We don't want to prove we are the best player in town, we just want all the money."[4]

Mason Malmuth wrote, "Once you reach a certain level of competence at poker, your most important decision by far is game selection."[5] If winners can't find a beatable game, they don't play. They apply an old adage, "It is no good to be the tenth best player in the world if the top nine are in your game."

Some moderately competent players become winners by playing only against weak players. I call them "walkers" because they walk around looking for soft games. If they don't find one, they keep walking.

The same principle applies to choosing the stakes. As the stakes get higher, the games get tougher. Winners realistically compare themselves to the competition and select the stakes that give them the most profitable edge. If a smaller game looks more profitable than their usual game, they change games.

Winners also look for games that favor their style of play. They keep records that teach them, for example, that they win more in

4. Konstantin Othmer, *The Elements of Seven Card Stud* (Cupertino, CA: Strategy One Publishing, 1989–92), 173.

5. Mason Malmuth, "The Best Game," in *Poker Essays,* 122. This same quotation was used in chapter 14 of this book.

shorthanded than full games or that they do poorly against very aggressive opponents. Then they play *only* in the right kind of games. Most players don't know which games favor them. They just take any open seat.

A few losers actually look for tough games. They regard poker as a macho contest, like the battle between Edward G. Robinson and Steve McQueen in *The Cincinnati Kid.* They played, not for just money, but for bragging rights, trying to prove who was better.

It is fun to watch such confrontations, but they rarely happen, at least not between winners. If there are enough weak players, they divide their money, while avoiding each other. It is not "professional courtesy." Winners just value money more than machismo. If there are too many good players, some of them implicitly say, "This game isn't big enough for all of us, so I'm leaving." It is not heroic, but winners value winning, not heroism.

Top players play against each other in tournaments, but they are essentially dividing the "dead money," the thousands or millions of dollars of weaker players' entry fees. Without dead money, many pros would avoid tournaments because it is not profitable to play against each other.

The weak players' dead money also drives the biggest games. The experts push chips back and forth, waiting for a rich fish. Barry Greenstein's "cash game play supports a lifestyle that costs more than $1 million per year. . . . [He says] you want to play with bad rich players because that is the best way to make the most money. I notice that a lot of younger players want to prove how good they are, and because of that they do not select good games. . . . To me poker is not about proving I can beat everyone. It is about paying the bills."[6]

---

6. Lizzy Harrison, "Capture the Flag," *Card Player,* May 21, 2008. Television shows have experts playing against each other, but they are *not* doing it for the money. See the discussion on pages 202–203.

Sports rhetoric encourages you to fight harder when the odds are against you. "When the going gets tough, the tough get going." "The team that won't be beaten, can't be beaten." These slogans are fine for games you must play, but they are absurd for poker. Leave them for the macho fools, and play in games you can beat.

Attack Weaker Players

Winners always see who has entered the pot before committing themselves, and they play hands differently against varied opponents. If a strong player is already in, they may fold cards they would normally play. If only weak players are in, they may raise to keep out the stronger ones. It is the exact opposite of chivalry, as if the knights avoided fighting each other because it was easier to beat up women and children.[7]

Of course, if they think they have the best hand, winners will attack anybody, but they need a much better hand to attack another winner. They know that winners have good cards and can play them well. They attack the weaker players because they often have poor cards and misplay them.

In tournaments, especially no-limit ones, winners exploit another form of weakness: the other players' stacks. In cash games you can buy more chips, but—unless you're in the rebuy period—if you lose your stack, you're finished.

If a player has a small stack, winners will attack him. They know that he can't hit back very hard and that he will fold some hands to survive. Conversely, they will be cautious against players with large

---

7. In fact, knights generally avoided each other because it was safer and more profitable to exploit peasants and merchants.

stacks. In no-limit tournaments anyone—even the worst fish—can bust someone with a smaller stack.[8]

Winners Consider All These Factors Before Making Commitments

Since they want the largest possible edge, they wait and wait and wait. They prefer to attack when they have the right combination of a soft game, a weak player, superior cards, and good position.

Most players don't have the patience and discipline to wait for the best moment. Some are so indecisive that they are afraid to attack, and they die a slow death by letting the aggressive players determine when and where they fight. Others yield to their ego or desire for action and fight battles they can't win. To be a winner, you have to *master your fears, your gambling impulses, and your ego, wait until you have the best of it, and then attack hard to make the most of it.*

Winners' Laws

Selective aggression should be the foundation of your own strategy. Select or create situations that give you an edge and then attack ferociously. You need extreme objectivity, discipline, and decisiveness to follow these Winners' Laws.

1. Accept that you *must* be selectively aggressive.

That acceptance is essential. Without it your emotions or irra-

---

8. With strong hands winners will try to isolate weak players with large stacks to double up.

tional motives can cause mistakes. Your desire to prove something about yourself or the urge to challenge tough players and situations can cause you to take foolish risks. Your fears can make you hesitant. Your desire to be fair or gentle can prevent you from exploiting your edge. Ignore these drives, get the edge, and then exploit it.

2. Honestly compare your abilities and style to the competition and situation.

You can't select the right times and places to attack without these comparisons. Since we already covered this principle, I won't discuss it now. Chapter 24 contains all your self-rating comparisons.

3. Select the games you have the best chance of beating.

If you select the wrong game, you're dead before you start. Don't try to prove something by playing in games that are too tough for you. Beatable games may not be as much fun, but the most basic of all trade-offs is fun versus profit. But don't overdo it. If you pick a game you detest just because you have a huge edge, you may not exploit that edge well. You may dislike the game so much that you can't play well, or the experience can be too unpleasant to tolerate. For example, you obviously have a huge edge against a bunch of drunks, but they may be so obnoxious that you hate playing and make mistakes.

4. Select the best times and places to attack.

Selecting the right game is an essential first step, but it's not enough. Within that game you must decide when and where to attack. If you do the right thing at the wrong time, you'll probably fail. Conversely, if your timing is right, you can probably get away with an imperfect strategy.

How Do You Rate?

These two rating scales measure the major components of selective aggression: (1) picking the right opportunities, and (2) attacking fiercely.

Picking the Right Opportunities

Circle the number that best describes your agreement with this statement: *I am very selectively aggressive. If I don't have an edge, I don't play.* (7) Agree strongly, (6) Agree, (5) Agree somewhat, (4) Neutral, (3) Disagree somewhat, (2) Disagree, (1) Disagree strongly.

Circle that number in the appropriate place on page 265.

Attacking Hard When You Have an Edge

Circle the number that best describes your agreement with this statement: *When I have an edge, I maximize its value by attacking ferociously.* (7) Agree strongly, (6) Agree, (5) Agree somewhat, (4) Neutral, (3) Disagree somewhat, (2) Disagree, (1) Disagree strongly.

Circle that number in the appropriate place in on page 265.

The Critical Questions

Review this chapter, especially the Winners' Laws and How Do You Rate? sections. Then answer two questions:

1. What are the implications of my self-ratings?
2. What should I do differently? List *specific actions* you should take to be more selectively aggressive.

Discuss your answers with someone you trust and take good notes.

21. Winners Push When They Are Winning

Many talented people . . . fail simply because they could not
leave a loser when they no longer had the best of it.
—**David Sklansky**[1]

Among the dumbest words in poker are, "I've got to get even," and you'll hear them again and again. Countless people—including some talented players—simply cannot accept losing, not even for one night, and they will do almost anything to get even. They often convert small losses into much larger or even catastrophic ones.

They become too emotional to see that losing is a sign that something may be wrong. Bad luck is often the primary cause for short-term losses but they may completely ignore other possibilities. For example, the game may be too tough for them, they may be playing badly, or their bad luck or their mistakes may have created a weak table image that encourages opponents to take shots at them. They may also have the irrational belief that "my luck has *got* to change."

An excessive need to get even causes some losers to go on tilt. Because they're so far behind, they can't get even by playing sensibly, so they become wildly aggressive. Some normally fine players have played so badly while on tilt that much weaker players easily beat them.

Winners rarely go on tilt for more than a minute or two because

1. David Sklansky, *Gambling for a Living* (Henderson, NV: Two Plus Two, 1997, 1998), 272.

they are brutally realistic about themselves. If they are too upset to play well, they take a walk, have lunch, talk to someone, or just go home. They know that there will always be another game and that they must preserve their bankrolls to exploit tomorrow's opportunities.

A few losers fall apart completely. If they are losing too much to get even in their current game, they move to a larger one, ignoring three critical facts:

1. Larger games are generally tougher.
2. They may not be playing their best.
3. If they are known as a lower-stakes player, their opponents may see them as weak and play more aggressively against them.

If their losses become too large, a few losers take more desperate gambles such as going to the craps table, playing roulette, or making large bets on horse races or sports, which are all −EV gambles. They usually just lose more heavily.

Winners don't get that desperate, nor do they think, 'I've *got* to get even.' They accept that bad beats and bad luck are just part of the game, and they do not feel much pressure to break even tonight. They focus on long-term results and accept that losing sessions, even losing months, are unavoidable. There will always be another game, and as long as they preserve their bankroll and personal equilibrium, they will end up winning.

This chapter expands the discussion of chapter 6. It states that winners focus on their expectation *now.* Trying to get even violates that principle because:

• Your decision is based on your previous losses, not your current expectation.

- Losing suggests (but does not prove) that your expectation is negative, while winning suggests it is positive.

You must resist the natural tendency to believe that your wins are caused by skill and your losses by bad luck. Losing often increases this self-deception. Since you don't want to believe that you're playing badly or that a game is too tough for you, you may exaggerate luck's effects. Force yourself to look objectively at what has happened, realistically compare your play to the competition's, and base the play or quit decision *entirely* on your current expectation.

Self-Fulfilling Prophecies

Winning and losing can be self-fulfilling prophecies. First, when you are winning, you may play more confidently and decisively. Second, your opponents may become timid and indecisive. They don't want to confront confident, decisive players, nor do they want to take on lucky ones.

Hitting and Running

In addition to playing too long and aggressively when losing, some losers "hit and run." If they get a little ahead, they quit to lock up their profits. It is exactly the wrong thing to do. "Quitting early when you are winning often means quitting when you are playing your best and your image is most effective, enabling you to win more easily."[2]

Conversely, when you are losing, you may play less decisively, and your opponents will tend to see you as weak and perhaps unlucky. They will be encouraged to attack, forcing you onto the de-

2. John Feeney, *Inside the Poker Mind* (Henderson, NV: Two Plus Two, 2000), 58.

fensive and reducing or eliminating any edge you may normally have.

For all these reasons, *winners push when they are winning, but become more conservative when they are losing.* If they are winning, they will stay in the game longer and play their cards more aggressively.

Playing the Rush

This term is used for a specific type of aggression. A "rush" occurs whenever someone wins several hands in a brief period, and winners push to exploit their rush. They play more hands, more aggressively. They push until opponents start counterattacking successfully. Sometimes, nobody pushes back, and the aggressor keeps rolling over everybody.

Doyle Brunson really plays the rush. In *Super System,* he wrote:

> If you're going to have a rush, you've got to . . . sustain that rush. . . . You've got to get in there and play. After I've won a pot in no-limit, I'm in the next pot, *regardless of what two cards I pick up.* I keep playing every pot until I lose one. And, in all those pots, I gamble more than I normally would.[3]

Does Doyle believe that his past cards affect future ones? I doubt it very much. He "plays the rush" aggressively, not because he expects better cards, but because apparent rushes scare people, and he is a master at exploiting that fear.

Although a rush will not affect your cards, many players will think that you're hot, and that belief will affect their play against you. . . . The more afraid they are, the more easily you can run over

3. Doyle Brunson, *Doyle Brunson's Super System: A Course in Power Poker* (NY: Cardoza, 2002) 450–451.

them. . . . For a brief time you will have a frightening table image, and you should take advantage of it, *but only with the players who fear you and your rush.* You can play a *few* more hands, be a *bit* more aggressive, and bluff a *little* more often. . . . Enjoy the rush, and take advantage of the table image it creates, but don't take foolish chances just because you think you're hot.[4]

Stu Ungar demonstrated fear's effects at the final table of the WSOP Championship. He had the largest stack, he was playing brilliantly, and everybody was afraid of him. Several observers said that everybody else was playing for second place. He raised repeatedly, and everyone folded.

You may ask, "What is the difference between Stu's raising almost every hand and a tilted player's playing the same way?" Stu's play had a huge positive expectation because of his *skill, image,* and *stack size.* He had the largest stack, he was seen as playing brilliantly, and everyone was afraid of him. Players on tilt are seen as fools, and others are *eager* to confront them.

Winners' Laws

This chapter won't have many Winners' Laws because the principles are very simple.

1. Push when you're winning.

2. Back off when you're losing.

These two rules are quite simple, but many people can't accept and apply them. Losing arouses such strong feelings that they can't

4. Alan Schoonmaker, "Playing the Rush," in *Your Best Poker Friend* (NY: Lyle Stuart, 2007), 131–134.

accept it. They lack the detachment and realism to accept that losing is just part of the game. And their fear of giving back their profits prevents them from getting the full value from their winning sessions.

3. Don't try too hard to "get even."

Since losing sessions are inevitable, you *must* learn how to cope with them or quit playing poker. Otherwise, you can go on tilt and lose *everything*. It has happened thousands of times.

4. Look hard at your own motives.

Why are you driven by the need to "get even"? You probably don't know, and you may refuse to accept that your motives are irrational. For example, you may be too egotistical to accept losing, especially to players you regard as inferior. If you don't understand your motives, your need to get even can destroy you.

How Do You Rate?

This rating scale measures your tendency to push when winning or losing.

Circle the number that best describes your agreement with this statement: *I push much harder when I am winning than when I am losing.* (7) Agree strongly, (6) Agree, (5) Agree somewhat, (4) Neutral, (3) Disagree somewhat, (2) Disagree, (1) Disagree strongly.

Circle that number in the appropriate place on page 265.

The Critical Questions

Review this chapter, especially the Winners' Laws and How Do You Rate? sections. Then answer two questions:

1. What are the implications of my self-ratings?
2. What should I do differently? List *specific actions* you
   should take to push harder when you are winning.

Discuss your answers with someone you trust and take good
notes.

22. Winners Adjust Effectively to Changes

You can't win without adjusting to the way a game is changing,

—**Matt Lessinger**[1]

Chapter 15 stated that winners use feedback loops well to correct errors and adjust to changes. The mental parts of the feedback loop (acquiring information, interpreting it, and revising your strategy) were covered in that chapter. These steps are essential, but worthless, if you don't act decisively to implement the revised strategy. Because poker constantly changes, you can't win without adjusting effectively to short- and long-term changes.

Losers don't adjust well. They don't get the right information, misinterpret it, refuse to revise their strategies, or don't act decisively.

The faster situations change, the more important adjusting rapidly becomes. If you don't adjust quickly enough, it may not matter what you do. You may make a costly mistake, or the window of opportunity may disappear. Adjusting rapidly is exceptionally important when you play online because you must act so quickly. Again, we see the clash between effectiveness and comfort. It is more comfortable to continue to do what you were doing, but not adjusting can wipe you out.

1. Matt Lessinger, personal communication to author, October 11, 2004.

Short-Term Changes

Poker situations change thousands of times every night. New cards are dealt every few seconds, and every one of them can completely change the situation. A poor hand (like a four-flush) becomes unbeatable, and a monster (like three aces) becomes worthless. The players holding every hand must adjust to the new situation. The lucky player should maximize his profits, whereas the unlucky ones should minimize their losses. And they all have only a few moments to adjust.

When one hand is over, a new one is dealt, and the players must shift their focus to it. Many losers can't do it; they brood about previous hands, which prevents them from playing *this* hand well. Winners may mentally replay hands, but their purpose is different: they compare the way this hand is being played to earlier hands to improve their understanding and strategy.

Position, a major source of power, changes frequently, sometimes (in stud) with every card. Winners adjust rapidly and well, while losers ignore or minimize position changes.

Your opponents are the most important factor, and all players combine consistency and change. They have a customary style such as tight-passive or loose-aggressive, but occasionally act out of character. The Rock may bluff because he thinks he can get away with it, is angry with someone, gets a wild impulse, or has gone on tilt. The Maniac may suddenly tighten up because he is short of money, is thinking about something else, or is just tired of losing. Obviously, you must adjust your strategy to fit their changed style. Winners continually adjust to the way others are playing *now*.

The number of players changes constantly as people take breaks, change tables, or go home. You must adjust your strategy.

For example, as the game gets short-handed, you must become looser and more aggressive.

Your entire game can change when one or two players leave and are replaced by very different ones. This problem is particularly acute for online players. In a cardroom you can easily see that a new player is in a seat, but online you have only a name and perhaps an icon. In addition, online players turn over very quickly, especially if you're multi-tabling.

If Maniacs replace Rocks, the game will be turned upside down. The Maniacs will raise and reraise almost every hand, creating huge pots and putting other players off-balance. If Rocks replace Maniacs, the entire game will tighten up. Anytime the game changes, your strategy should change. The strategy that worked well just a few minutes ago may become utterly inappropriate.

Long-Term Changes

The "long-term" has gotten much shorter recently. Until a few years ago, major changes occurred slowly, but television, online poker, and an explosion of books, DVDs, coaching websites, and computer software have changed poker more in the past few years than in the previous fifty.

These changes have caused a "Darwinian" evolution.[2] Because draw and five-card stud have almost disappeared, professionals who made their living from them had to switch to hold'em, Omaha, and seven-card stud. In the past few years, no limit hold'em has become the fashionable game, seven-card stud has nearly disap-

---

2. The next few paragraphs are based on pages 205–262 of *Your Worst Poker Enemy* (NY: Lyle Stuart, 2007). Because I mixed direct quotations and paraphrasing, I have omitted quotation marks.

peared, and soft middle-limit hold'em games are hard to find. The professionals have had to change games again.

In all games some losers learn how to play. Other losers go broke, get discouraged, or give up for other reasons. New players replace them, and—thanks to training aids—many of them quickly shift from clueless, to not bad, to competent, or even better. Because the weakest players leave and the survivors improve, the competition gets tougher, and only players who continually develop themselves can win. Darwin called this process "the survival of the fittest."

When I started playing, there were hardly any books, nor were there any good magazines. The "classics," such as *The Education of a Poker Player, Oswald Jacoby on Poker,* and *Scarne's Guide to Modern Poker,* offered "expert advice" that is primitive by modern standards. If you blindly followed their recommendations today, you would be slaughtered.

And most players did not even read them! They went to "the school of hard knocks," and it has always charged high tuition and taken a long time to graduate. You had to lose a lot of money and play for a long time to learn how to play well.

Today you can get *Card Player* every two weeks, study a new book or DVD every day, and discuss poker hands and theory every night on Internet forums. Instead of relying on dubious information and learning through experience, you can get excellent advice, and much of it is based on data that did not exist until recently.

For example, you can run computer simulations on your own PC, and you can read analyses based on simulations. You can also read books based on the analysis of over 1,000,000 actual hands.[3]

3. See, for example, Nick (Stoxtrader) Grudzien and Geoff (Zobags) Herzog, *Winning in Tough Hold'em Games: Short-Handed and High-Stakes Concepts and Theory for Limit Hold'em* (Henderson, NV: Two Plus Two, 2007).

There is no substitute for experience, but these new tools speed up the learning curve, making the competition tougher.

You *must* continue to improve just to survive. If you play the same way tomorrow that you did today, your results will slowly deteriorate. Every large cardroom has former winners in large games who now struggle to survive in small ones. They probably reject responsibility and blame other factors, but it's their fault for not developing their game. They didn't realize poker was changing until it was too late.

> Computers have already had dramatic effects on other games such as backgammon. Dan Harrington, WSOP Champion and primary author of the *Harrington on Hold'em* books, told me that he was once a world-class backgammon player. He stopped playing for several years and then started again. He used the new computer tools that had come out during his absence. He told me, "I was unquestionably a much better player than I had been before, but I was no longer world class. The game had advanced more than I had."
>
> The same process will happen in poker. Because of research using these online data pools and other resources, poker strategy will continue to advance. The last word has not been written about poker (or any other subject), and it never will be written.[4]

Continuing Professional Education

Many professionals such as doctors, lawyers, and psychologists can't renew their licenses unless they take continuing education courses. Because legislators know how complacent people can be, they insist that professionals continually work on self-

---

4. Alan Schoonmaker, *Your Worst Poker Enemy,* 237.

development. Without that requirement many professionals would not develop themselves.

Becoming a poker winner is much more difficult than succeeding as a licensed professional. Nearly all professionals make a living, but most poker players lose, and only a tiny number win enough to support themselves. If you want to become or continue to be a winner, *you must take your professional education seriously.*

Winners' Laws

1. Accept that the only constant is change.

You may not like that fact, but it is unquestionably true. If you deny that reality, you will certainly get some nasty surprises.

2. Ask frequently: "How is my game changing?"

Read *Card Player* and other sources to learn how poker is generally changing. Continually monitor your own game for specific changes such as the number of players, the way each one plays, and the way each one adapts to changing conditions.

3. Think frequently of how to adjust to these changes.

Don't wait until the last moment. If you do, you can't act in a deliberate, controlled way. Instead, think ahead, planning the specific actions you will take and the time and way that you will take them. The final chapter contains some general suggestions, but you need to be much more specific.

4. Develop the knowledge and skills you will need *before* you need them.

You can't win tomorrow's battles with yesterday's weapons and strategies. Don't wait until change has passed you by, and then try to catch up. Anticipate tomorrow's demands and get ready for them in advance. Force your opponents to catch up to you.

5. When you see that change is needed, *do it!*

Recognizing the need for change is the essential first step, but it's worthless without decisive action. No matter how reluctant you are, *you must make those changes*!

How Do You Rate?

The next two rating scales measure your self-assessment of the two main skills: (1) recognizing the need to change; (2) adjusting quickly and effectively.

Recognizing the Need to Change

Circle the number that best describes your agreement with this statement: *I am exceptionally good at recognizing the need to change.* (7) Agree strongly, (6) Agree, (5) Agree somewhat, (4) Neutral, (3) Disagree somewhat, (2) Disagree, (1) Disagree strongly.

Circle that number in the appropriate place on page 266.

Adjusting Quickly and Effectively

Circle the number that best describes your agreement with this statement: *After seeing the need to change, I am exceptionally good at adjusting quickly and effectively.* (7) Agree strongly, (6) Agree, (5) Agree somewhat, (4) Neutral, (3) Disagree somewhat, (2) Disagree, (1) Disagree strongly.

Circle that number in the appropriate place on page 266.

The Critical Questions

Review this chapter, especially the Winners' Laws and How Do You Rate? sections. Then answer two questions:

1. What are the implications of my self-rating?
2. What should I do differently? List *specific actions* you should take to adjust more effectively to changes.

Discuss your answers with someone you trust and take good notes.

23. Winners Pay Their Dues

Be a student of the game.... Treat it like you are weight lifting, making yourself stronger, day after day, year after year.

—**Roy Cooke**

Roy Cooke gave that answer when I asked, "What's the best advice you can give to our listeners?" Roy, Barry Tanenbaum, Mark Gregorich, and Don Olney were guests on Lou Krieger's roundersradio .com show, "Keep Flopping Aces."[1] All four have been successful pros for over a decade, and they were discussing the general question, "Should you turn pro?" Although they did not use the term, they clearly stated that you should not turn pro unless you are willing and able to pay your dues.

Paying them is far from easy. Real pros make most of the trade-offs described in the previous chapters. They deliberately sacrifice time, energy, fun, excitement, socialization, and general comfort to maximize their profits.

At the table they study their opponents, monitor their own play, control their emotions, and so on. And they *act* like professionals. After the show Tanenbaum told me he once saw Cooke taking beat after beat. "You never would have known he was losing heavily from his play or conversation. He kept playing well, and he seemed as relaxed and friendly as usual."

When they aren't playing, pros work on their games. They read books, including ones they dislike. They want to understand how

---

1. I was guest host because Lou was on vacation. You can hear the entire program at roundersradio.com. Click on "Podcasts," "Keep Flopping Aces," and "5/29/08."

their opponents think. Some of them write lengthy notes about opponents, and—if an opponent has been on television—they record and intensely analyze the shows.

They constantly review their own play and get feedback from coaches, poker buddies, discussion groups, and online forums. They know many talented players who failed as pros because they did not work hard enough or do the other unpleasant and unnatural things that real pros do. In simplest terms, *most people play poker, but pros work at it.*

You Must Pay Your Dues

Even if you aren't turning pro, you must still pay your dues to be a winner. The tasks discussed in the previous chapters are parts of your dues, and the more of them you do, the bigger winner you will be. Work especially hard on the ones you dislike because you probably don't do them very well.[2]

Countless talented players are losers because they didn't pay their dues. They relied on their natural talent, but it just wasn't enough, nor will your talent make you a winner without working hard.

Some young players are surprised when they are told that they must work hard to become winners. Because of the "Build Self-Esteem Movement," their parents and teachers didn't demand that they work for praise, grades, or money, and they see no reason to work hard to beat poker. They implicitly regard winning as an "entitlement," almost a constitutional right. They want to do whatever they enjoy doing, but still beat our extremely tough game.

The "Entitlement Mentality" is everywhere. A Google search got

---

2. The cause and effect relationship is ambiguous. You may not do them well because you dislike them, you may dislike them because you don't do them well, or both.

over 21,000 hits, and it affects virtually every aspect of modern life. Students, workers, wives, husbands, taxpayers, older people, younger people, welfare recipients, and even criminals sincerely believe "I'm entitled" to this, that, or the other thing.

This expectation is alien to poker winners. They all know that only hard-working, disciplined people survive poker's ferocious competition. Many young people don't believe them. They think it is easy or that it *should* be easy. Why should they have to work hard to win at poker when they never worked hard for anything else?

Tommy Angelo succinctly summarized the winners' attitude toward the entitlement mentality. "No matter how good you play, or how bad they play, you are not entitled to win. If you have time and money, you are entitled to a seat at the table. That is all."[3]

What Dues Must You Pay?

Attitudes are not the only problem. You may not know what your dues are. To become a doctor, lawyer, CPA, or psychologist you must get a specific degree, work thousands of hours under supervision, pass certain exams, and so on. If you don't satisfy every requirement, you can't practice.

There are no formal requirements in poker, and *your* dues depend on your Personal Definition of Winning.[4] The more ambitious your goals are, the larger your dues will be. For example, you can't become a top player without *committing* yourself wholeheartedly to poker.

Since the dues are not clearly defined, you may have to work very hard to learn what they are. Earlier chapters described *some* of the dues, and the next few paragraphs summarize the basic require-

3. Tommy Angelo (*Elements of Poker*; Privately published, 2007), 75.

4. See pages 39–40.

ments, but—if your goals are ambitious—you should go much further.

First and most important, *you must thoroughly understand poker.* Not too long ago, that understanding could come only from experience and face-to-face discussions because there weren't many good books, other instructional materials, and online forums. But now there are many good books, videos, DVDs, online forums, and other sources of excellent information and advice. Many poker winners—even ones who aren't full-time pros—study almost as hard as members of traditional professions.

Second, *you must get a great deal of winning experience.* You must prove that you can beat smaller games before moving to larger ones. The competition gets tougher as the stakes get larger. Merely winning briefly is *not* proof that you are ready to move up because you may just have been lucky.

Third, *you should move up slowly and develop the skills you need to succeed at each level before moving further.* It is very foolish to jump from low stakes such as $1–$2 to middle limits such as $10–$20, and it is suicidal to jump from low stakes to high ones such as $100–$200. Yet every large cardroom has losing middle- and high-stakes players who never consistently beat even tiny games. They offer all sorts of rationalizations for moving up:

- They find small games boring.
- They believe players in small games aren't smart enough to respect their skill.
- They can read good players, but not bad ones, because they don't know what they're doing.

All those rationalizations are nonsense. If you can't beat bad players, you can't beat better ones.

The Skills Hierarchy

Just beating small games does *not* mean that you can beat larger ones. The skills required change dramatically as you move up. Barry Tanenbaum pointed out that there is

a rough hierarchy of skills. As you move from easy games to tougher games . . . you need to develop new skills. . . .

[An] evolution of skills happens in poker. A player may start out playing tight, and win against loose opponents. If he tries to move up to more advanced games, he will find that everyone can play selectively, and he needs to add skills to continue to win. . . . They then chose to utilize the skills best suited for the particular game they find themselves in.[5]

Even if you don't intend to turn pro, you should read Tanenbaum's articles. I will just repeat three of his points.

1. Bigger, tougher games require considerably different skills from smaller ones.
2. Only people who have developed *all* these skills can succeed.
3. These skills should be developed in a logical order.

Other Costs of Not Paying Your Dues

Not paying your dues can also wipe out your bankroll. Some people have whined, "I won steadily for six months, moving up

5. Barry Tanenbaum, "Where Does One Big Bet Per Hour Come From?" Parts I and II, *Poker Pages*, www.pokerpages.com/articles/archives/tanenbaum04.htm.

from $1–$2 to $2–$4 to $5–$10 to $10–$20, building my bankroll, but in just two weeks it was gone. How could that happen?"

They want sympathy, but they got exactly what they deserved. They may or may not have developed all the skills needed to win at higher limits, but they certainly had not built a large enough bankroll. Mason Malmuth demonstrated that a great Texas Hold'em player needs about $3,900 to survive at $10–$20; a good player needs about $4,900, and an okay player needs about $8,000.[6] Many whiners did not have enough skill or experience to beat their games, and their bankrolls were much too small. In fact, some of them rejected the entire concept of conservative bankroll management. Perhaps other people needed such large bankrolls, but *they* did not.

The whiners lack the toughness and emotional maturity that can come only from lots of experience and study. If they had paid their dues, they would realize that they moved up too rapidly and that they did not have the bankroll to succeed at $10–$20. They would also have learned that *nobody* goes forever without a losing streak. Losing streaks, even lengthy ones, are just parts of the game, and winners build the bankrolls and the emotional toughness they need before moving upward.

One reason I love poker is that I detest the entitlement mentality. I believe it has had disastrous economic, social, and psychological effects. People who insist, "I'm entitled," may be rewarded in other places, but they are usually punished at the poker table. If you think that you're entitled to win, poker is the wrong game for you. Conversely, if you accept the responsibility to pay your dues, you'll win more than equally talented players who refuse to pay them.

---

6. Mason Malmuth, "What Your Bankroll Should Be," *Poker Essays* (Henderson, NV: Two Plus Two, 1991), 58.

Winners' Laws

Most writers about the entitlement mentality complain about its negative effects. I agree with these complaints, but it creates great opportunities *if you don't share it.* Just apply these Winners Laws to ensure that you pay your dues and exploit those who won't pay them.

1. Accept that you *must* pay your dues.

You may have some of that entitlement mentality. You may feel that you deserve to win because you're so talented or just because you're a great person. Forget it. The more you think that way, the worse long-term results you'll get.

2. Learn what the dues really are.

You may have to work very hard to learn what they are but learning them is essential. This book is just a starting point. You should go much further.

3. Learn how to pay them.

Learn what you must do to develop the necessary skills and personal qualities. Read about people with similar ambitions and ask ones who have succeeded what they did.

4. Make a plan for paying your dues.

Your plan should state how and when you will pay each one. The next chapter will discuss some steps you should take.

How Do You Rate?

We will assess two qualities: (1) your attitude toward paying your dues; (2) your ability to pay them.

Your Attitude Toward Paying Dues

Circle the number that best describes your agreement with this statement: *I completely accept that I have to pay my dues.* (7) Agree strongly, (6) Agree, (5) Agree somewhat, (4) Neutral, (3) Disagree somewhat, (2) Disagree, (1) Disagree strongly.

Insert that number in the appropriate place on page 266.

Your Knowledge and Ability to Pay Your Dues

They are independent, but we will combine them into one rating scale. Circle the number that best describes your agreement with this statement: *I know what the dues are, and I can pay them.* (7) Agree strongly, (6) Agree, (5) Agree somewhat, (4) Neutral, (3) Disagree somewhat, (2) Disagree, (1) Disagree strongly.

Circle that number in the appropriate place on page 266.

The Critical Questions

Review this chapter, especially the Winners' Laws and How Do You Rate? sections. Then answer two questions:

1. How can I learn what dues I must pay?
2. What should I do to pay my dues?

Discuss your answer with someone you trust and take good notes.

24. How to Become a Winner

The previous chapters have thoroughly described the differences between winners and other players. I hope you have compared yourself to winners by completing all the self-ratings and inserted them into this chapter.

The Winners' Laws in those chapters were specific recommendations for applying each chapter's principles. This chapter goes a large step further. It will help you do the following:

- Compare your overall profile to the winners' profile.
- Break out of your comfort zone to become a winner (or a bigger one).

After reading this chapter, a friend said, "Most people won't do all the work you recommend." He is right, but most poker players are losers. And the biggest reason they lose is that they won't pay their dues. If you really want to be one of the few winners, you have to *work*.

The "How Do You Rate?" Data

Every chapter except the introductions included some rating scales. To make it easier to compare yourself to the winners' profile, we will record all your data here.

Please circle your answer in the appropriate place below.

In many chapters you may have written answers to Critical Questions. It will often be helpful to look at those answers, but they are not written here. The immediate goal is to help you see the overall comparison between your own profile and the winners' profile.

The most important ratings are the ones in chapters 2, 3, and 4. They will affect many of the ratings from other chapters.

Seeing your profile should help you identify your most important assets and liabilities. The ratings higher than four are assets, while the lower ones are liabilities. The numerical ratings mean:

7 = Agree strongly

6 = Agree

5 = Agree somewhat

4 = Neutral

3 = Disagree somewhat

2 = Disagree

1 = Disagree strongly

PART 1: Introduction

Chapter 2: Winners Are More Motivated and Disciplined
This chapter has two self-rating scales:

Your Motivation
While playing poker, I am
intensely competitive. I will do
almost anything to maximize my
profits.   7   6   5   4   3   2   1

Your Discipline

While playing poker, I am
extremely disciplined. I can
control myself no matter what
happens.

7   6   5   4   3   2   1

Chapter 3: Winners Make Good Trade-Offs

This chapter did not have the same format. It asked, "Why Do
You Play Poker?" It also had a series of ratings of specific trade-offs.

Why Do You Play Poker?

Make money   ____%

Socialize, meet people   ____%

Relax   ____%

Get excitement of gambling   ____%

Test yourself against tough competition   ____%

Develop your skills   ____%

Get sense of accomplishment from winning   ____%

Get status and fame   ____%

Pass time   ____%

Other (specify)   ____%

_____   ____%

_____   ____%

_____   ____%

Total (must be 100%)   ____%

Specific Trade-offs

Profits vs. Fun

	Profits					Fun	
	7	6	5	4	3	2	1

Profits vs. Avoiding Frustrations

	Profits				Avoiding Frustration		
	7	6	5	4	3	2	1

Rewards vs. Risks

	Risks					Profits	
	7	6	5	4	3	2	1

Profits vs. Variance

	Profits					Variance	
	7	6	5	4	3	2	1

Profits vs. Fame and Status

Profits				Fame and Status		
7	6	5	4	3	2	1

Profits vs. Testing Yourself Against Tough Competition

Profits				Testing Yourself		
7	6	5	4	3	2	1

Profits vs. Developing Your Skills

Profits (immediate)				Developing Your Skills		
7	6	5	4	3	2	1

Profits vs. Affection

Profits				Affection		
7	6	5	4	3	2	1

Profits vs. Being Deceptive and Exploitative

Profits				Being Deceptive and Exploitative		
7	6	5	4	3	2	1

Profits vs. Ego Building

Profits				Ego Building		
7	6	5	4	3	2	1

Chapter 4: Winners Manage Risks and Information Very Well

I am neither a risk seeker nor a
risk avoider. While playing poker,
I always try to get the best of it
and to make the most of it.   7 6 5 4 3 2 1

Part Two: Winners Control Their Focus

Chapter 5: Winners Focus on Long-Term Results

While playing poker, I am
extremely focused on long-term
results. I nearly ignore short-term
rewards and punishments.   7 6 5 4 3 2 1

Chapter 6: Winners Focus on the Here and Now

While playing poker, I focus
completely on what I must do
here and now to get the best long-
term results.   7 6 5 4 3 2 1

Chapter 7: Winners Focus on Power

While playing poker, I focus
entirely on power and ignore luck,
morality, personal relationships,
and so on.   7 6 5 4 3 2 1

Chapter 8: Winners Focus on Other People

While playing poker, I focus on
other people, not myself.   7 6 5 4 3 2 1

Chapter 9: Winners Consider Complexities

When making important poker
decisions, I try to consider every
important factor, including ones I
dislike thinking about.   7 6 5 4 3 2 1

Part Three: Winners Control Their Thought Processes

Chapter 10: Winners Are Brutally Realistic

While playing poker, I am brutally
realistic. I work hard to prevent
my wishes and biases from
distorting my perceptions.   7 6 5 4 3 2 1

Chapter 11: Winners Think Logically

While playing poker, I always
emphasize logic. I never just "trust
my instincts."   7 6 5 4 3 2 1

Chapter 12: Winners Prepare Thoroughly

I prepare extremely thoroughly
for poker. I try to anticipate
contingencies and to make plans
to deal with all of them.   7 6 5 4 3 2 1

Chapter 13: Winners Concentrate Intensely

While playing poker, I always
concentrate intensely.   7 6 5 4 3 2 1

Chapter 14: Winners Probe Efficiently

I probe exceptionally well; I time
probes well and use many probing
techniques.   7   6   5   4   3   2   1

Chapter 15: Winners Use Feedback Loops Well

I am exceptionally good at using
feedback loops. I always regard
my first conclusion as tentative,
actively seek contradictory
information, and never reject
alternatives just because I "have
the courage of my convictions."   7   6   5   4   3   2   1

Part Four: Winners Control the Information They Transmit

Chapter 16: Winners Are Judiciously Deceptive

Winning is so important to me
that I always base my choice
between straightforward and
deceptive play on the effects on
my long-term profits.   7   6   5   4   3   2   1

Chapter 17: Winners Create the Right Images

I minimize my other motives and
do my best to project the image
that gives me the biggest edge.   7   6   5   4   3   2   1

Part Five: Winners Control Their Reactions to Feelings

Chapter 18: Winners Accept Poker As It Is

I accept poker completely as it is,
and I accept full responsibility for
my results.   7 6 5 4 3 2 1

Chapter 19: Winners Depersonalize Conflicts

I never take poker conflicts
personally or get angry about
them.   7 6 5 4 3 2 1

Part Six: Winners Act Decisively

Chapter 20: Winners Are Selectively Aggressive

This chapter has two self-rating scales:

Picking the right opportunities
I am very selectively aggressive. If
I don't have an edge, I don't play.   7 6 5 4 3 2 1

Attacking hard when you have an edge
When I have an edge, I maximize
its value by attacking ferociously.   7 6 5 4 3 2 1

Chapter 21: Winners Push When They Are Winning

I push much harder when I am
winning than when I am losing.   7 6 5 4 3 2 1

Chapter 22: Winners Adjust Effectively to Changes

This chapter has two self-rating scales:

Recognizing the need to change
I am exceptionally good at
recognizing the need to change.   7 6 5 4 3 2 1

Adjusting quickly and effectively
After seeing the need to change, I
am exceptionally good at
adjusting quickly and effectively.   7 6 5 4 3 2 1

Chapter 23: Winners Pay Their Dues

This chapter has two self-rating scales.

Your attitude toward paying dues
I completely accept that I have to
pay my dues.   7 6 5 4 3 2 1

Your knowledge and ability to pay your dues
I know what the dues are, and I
can pay them   7 6 5 4 3 2 1

After looking at all your self-ratings, you may feel discouraged because your profile is far from ideal. This feeling is normal, but it is actually a positive. It means that you are honestly self-critical. You recognize your liabilities, which is the indispensable first step toward overcoming them.

Nobody—not even the biggest winner—has the ideal profile. In fact, if you gave yourself all 7s and 6s, you are probably kidding yourself. Those statements are deliberately extreme: "I always . . ." "I never . . ." Hardly anyone always does the right thing, or never does the wrong one. We are humans, not machines.

You have been honest with yourself about where you are, and

you should be equally honest about the difficulty of changing yourself. You may want to move quickly, but it would be a huge mistake. If your plans are too ambitious, you will almost certainly become discouraged and make hardly any progress.

Your central problem is that making almost any significant change takes you out of your comfort zone. Because the same factors that shaped your basic personality created your comfort zone, breaking out of it is *extremely* difficult. The problems of breaking out of it are discussed in appendix C, and I urge you to read it.

What Steps Should You Take to Change Yourself?

These steps may seem too small and slow moving, but you are trying to make a very difficult change. Since most self-development programs fail, try something new.

Step One: Carefully select someone to help you. You may be surprised that this step comes first, but you really need that help. Without it you probably won't take the other steps well (or at all). Dr. Daniel Kessler, a clinical psychologist, made this point forcefully:

> Any change is difficult. . . . Even when people make a concerted effort to change, they generally succeed in the short term, then fail in the long term.
>
> It is close to impossible to do on your own. Outside help . . . will likely be needed. Sure, you may be able to do it on your own, but it is far more difficult. . . . Having someone to be accountable to is a significant element of success, as is the ability of an outside observer to see and comment on what you might not see.[1]

1. Dr. Daniel Kessler, e-mail message to author, March 25, 2008.

An outsider will help you understand yourself and the process; more importantly, he will reinforce your "conscience" or "willpower." You may think that you don't need that reinforcement, and that your own determination and willpower will make you stick to the program, but *self-improvement programs fail because people cheat.*

Most self-improvement programs would work if people stuck to them, but they just don't do it. Dieters eat snacks, smokers sneak cigarettes, exercisers cut corners. You will be less likely to cheat if someone else is watching you and the actions are easily counted.[2]

You can work with a poker buddy, but you will probably get better results with a professional coach.

- He knows more about how to improve your game.
- He has the experience to help you be honest and thorough.
- He charges you a fee, so you will probably take his advice more seriously. People usually ignore free advice.

Discuss every step with your coach or poker buddy. Ask him to help you pick the right change, identify the forces preventing it, and so on.

Step Two: Pick *one small, specific* change. Look over all your self-ratings in The "How Do You Rate?" Data section at the start of this chapter. Those self-ratings will suggest many changes you should make, but select only one. If you try to do too much, you will probably fail and become discouraged.

2. Weight Watchers, which is more successful than most programs, reduces cheating by having members *publicly* weigh themselves. People may insist, "I didn't cheat," but the scales don't lie.

By setting a "Mission"[3] to make *only* this change, you increase the probability that you will (1) take this action more often; (2) increase your understanding of how psychological factors damage your play; (3) overcome some of these psychological factors; (4) create confidence that you can make other changes.

Select a change with most of these characteristics. They are in their approximate order of importance.

- It must be an *action* because you can't really tell whether you've changed your thoughts or feelings.
- Pick an action that is relatively easy to take. For example, it is much easier to make a bluff raise than to change your reaction to a bad beat.
- You can easily count how often you do it.
- You *really* want to make it. Without a strong desire you probably won't do it.
- You believe this change will improve your play and long-term results. Without this belief you probably won't do it.
- It is not too far outside your comfort zone. If it will make you too uncomfortable, you may try it once or twice, but you probably won't stick with it.
- You are confident you can make it. If you don't think you can do it, you can't, but the opposite is not true. Confidence increases your chances of success, but doesn't guarantee it.
- You don't do it often enough partly because it makes you uncomfortable.
- You will get many opportunities to do it. You need to do it again and again to overcome the psychological forces inhibiting you.

3. Mike Caro coined the term "mission," and this approach is based on his concept.

Step Three: Commit yourself wholeheartedly to making this change. Commitment can make your feelings work for you. As David Sklansky put it, "One way to harness your feelings to give yourself willpower is to take great *pride* when you stick to a resolution, and to feel great *shame* when you don't."[4]

Step Four: Identify the psychological forces that prevent you from taking this action. Since you know you should do it more often, some psychological factors are inhibiting you. Try to determine what they are by asking yourself questions like this:

- Why haven't you been acting this way?
- Have you tried unsuccessfully to make this change?
- Why didn't it work?
- Are you afraid of feeling stupid if you make a mistake?
- What would make it easier for you to make this change?

You may realize that the forces against the change you selected are too powerful to overcome immediately. If so, select an easier one. For example, if asking questions while playing a hand makes you too uncomfortable, ask gentler, more open-ended questions after the hand is over. If check-raise bluffing is too difficult, bluff more when you have position.

Step Five: Accept in advance that you will pay a short-term price. You will certainly feel uncomfortable, and you may lose some money, perhaps a lot of it. Since short-term rewards and punishments have much greater impact than long-term ones, think differently about time. It's "merely a dimension. . . . Time is just another

4. David Sklansky, "Will Power," in *Fighting Fuzzy Thinking in Poker, Gaming, and Life* (Henderson, NV: Two Plus Two, 2000), 22.

way of specifying where you are. . . . Think of the rewards of your will power [as] not occurring in the future, but simply at another place."[5]

You are paying a small price here to get a much larger reward there. You *must* accept that price before starting. If you are surprised by it or if it really bothers you, you will probably cheat or even give up.

Step Six: Select situations that reduce your resistance to change. Your resistance goes down as the risks get smaller and the probability of success gets larger. Even if you dislike playing online, you should seriously consider experimenting while playing online for lower stakes than usual:

- The financial risks are obviously lower.
- Psychological risks are closely linked to financial ones. You will be less upset by losing a small amount than a larger one.
- Your psychological risks are also reduced by anonymity. If you make a mistake in a live game—especially with people you know well—you may feel embarrassed, particularly if they say something critical. You can play online with strangers and use a screen name. If you turn off chat, you won't even know what people are saying about you.
- You will get more chances to experiment because the games are so fast. You can even multi-table to multiply your opportunities.
- You can keep much better records, especially if you use hand-tracking software.

5. Sklansky, *Fighting Fuzzy Thinking*, 22.

If you won't play online, at least consider playing for smaller stakes than usual to reduce your risks. Regardless of where you play, experiment *only* when the risks are low and the probability of success is high. Let's say you want to make a specific aggressive play such as raising on the flop with a draw to get a free card on the turn. You'll lower your risks and increase the probability and value of succeeding by doing it:

- When you are against passive players.
- When nobody is behind you.

By picking good situations, you will increase both your chances to succeed and your confidence that you can do it.

Step Seven: Set a goal for the number of times you will take this action. This goal should be more than usual, but easily achievable (to increase your confidence). Achievable goals for a four-hour session, could be to:

- Check-raise bluff twice.
- Always fold suited connectors ten-nine or smaller in early position.
- Never open-limp.
- Ask questions while playing a hand at least three times.

Step Eight: Record the number of times that you take this action and how you felt while and after taking it. You can use chips to keep track of how many opportunities you have and how often you take this action. Just put a chip to the right for each opportunity and to the left for each time you take the action. Use a small notebook or index cards to keep long-lasting records of your actions, thoughts, and feelings. Without written records, your selective memory will probably cause mistakes.

Pay particular attention to the times that you took this action and wished you had not done it. For example, if you folded nine-eight suited and would have won a huge pot, how did you feel? If you asked a question and got a nasty answer, what did you feel and do?

Step Nine: Analyze your actions, thoughts, and feelings. After the session is over, carefully analyze your notes and discuss them with someone else. Ask why you reached or didn't reach your goal.

Pay particular attention to your feelings. Remember, they are the reason that you have not been doing what you know you should do. Look for changes in your feelings. Perhaps you were extremely uncomfortable the first time, but less uncomfortable later. If you see that it is getting easier, you will be more likely to continue.

Step Ten: Follow up this exercise. If you did not achieve your goal, set a more achievable one. You could try to check-raise bluff only once (versus your original goal of twice). Or you could fold all suited connectors nine-eight or smaller in early position (versus your original goal of folding suited connectors ten-nine or smaller). Set a goal you can reach to increase your confidence that you can change.

If you achieved your goal, set a slightly more ambitious one for a similar exercise. Exploit and increase your confidence and momentum by becoming a *little* more ambitious. Don't get cocky. You're still the same person, and those psychological forces are far from dead. You can become more ambitious in many ways. For example, you can:

- Increase the number of times you will take the same action such as check-raise bluffing three times (versus your original goal of twice).
- Find another way to tighten up in early position such as folding all pairs smaller than eights (versus your original goal of folding suited connectors ten-nine or smaller).
- Take the same action in slightly less favorable situations such as trying to check-raise bluff better players.

Your overall goal should be to change your game *slowly* from the one that makes you comfortable to one that produces bigger profits.

Step Eleven: Forgive yourself. Barry Tanenbaum's "Epilogue" is subtitled "Forgive Yourself."[6] When I first saw that subtitle, I was shocked. Had my old friend gotten religion or joined some New Age, touchy-feely group?

After reading and discussing it with him, I realized how right he was to end his book that way. So I will end this book with the same point. To improve your game, you *must* experiment with new ways of thinking and acting, and some of them will cause painful mistakes. If you can't forgive yourself, you will dwell on those mistakes and become unwilling to take essential risks. As Tanenbaum put it:

Whenever you play poker, you will make errors. As you expand your game . . . you will make more.

Of course, you will also get some right, and your overall results will improve. However, the wrong ones can cause you to doubt or even to blame yourself. You will think, "If only I did not play that

6. Barry Tanenbaum, *Advanced Limit Hold'em Strategy* (West Sussex, UK: D & B Publishing, 2007), 246.

hand (or make that raise or run that bluff or call that bet), I would not have lost that money."

The most important thing to remember is the need to forgive yourself. . . . The better you get at not dwelling on past mistakes other than to learn from them and move on, the better your play will be.

The choice is yours. You can continue in your safe, comfortable rut, or you can take the financial and psychological risks of experimenting with new ways of playing. It won't be easy, but you *can* break out of your comfort zone by experimenting, making mistakes, forgiving yourself, and repeating that cycle.

It won't be easy, but with this step-by-step approach, *you can develop the skills and attitudes you need to become a bigger winner.*

Appendixes

Appendix A: Answers to Questions in Chapter 1

I don't claim that these answers are right because—as you have often heard—"everything depends on the situation." I just want to help you to look at your decisions in a different way.

Situation A

A winner would want nine opponents because he would get the greatest long-term profits. Most players—and a surprising number of poker writers (who should know better)—would say "One or two" because the chances of winning go down with each additional caller. That argument is irrelevant from a profit-maximizing perspective.

With one opponent with random cards you would win about 85 percent of the time, and your percentage would go down with each additional caller, becoming 30 percent with nine of them. That's frustrating, but the long-term profits on your infrequent victories will be much greater. Let's look at playing 100 hands with one versus nine opponents.

With one opponent your aces would win $8,500 on the 85 winning hands and lose $1,500 on the 15 losing hands. The net profit would be $7,000 ($8,500 - $1,500).

With nine opponents your aces would win about 30 times for a total of $27,000 ($900 per hand times 30 hands). They would lose about 70 times for a total of $7,000 ($100 per hand times 70 hands). The net profit would be $20,000 ($27,000 - $7,000).

That $20,000 is nearly *triple* the $7,000 your aces would win heads-up, and a return of 200 percent on the $10,000 wagered. The people who whine, "I can't beat bad players because they call with anything," don't know what they're talking about. They are expressing their frustration because it hurts *now,* and the long-term profits are just an abstraction to them.[1]

But poker and this book are all about maximizing long-term profits. So keep reading to learn how to increase *your* long-term profits.

Situation B

A winner would ignore the drunk, keep playing a solid game, but adjust to his wild play and its effects on the other players. The game is soft, and many players are off-balance. If you play well, you have a very positive expectation.

You may be tempted to tell him he is an idiot or to explain why you play such a solid game, but they would be *terrible* mistakes. You could create a nasty argument, and you might drive him away or cause him or another player(s) to play more sensibly. Explaining how you play would give away information that could help *any* opponent to beat you. *Don't give away information!*

Don't change tables or go home unless he upsets you so much that you can't stand to play with him. If you're in danger of going on tilt, you should leave. Otherwise stay there and beat this soft game.

Loosening up would be extremely foolish, especially if you are trying to prove something. That desire often causes silly mistakes. Regardless of your reasons, loosening up can cause heavier losses. You may then go on tilt and take a terrible beating.

1. This example is from pages 171–172 of my book *The Psychology of Poker.* Because of some changes, I have omitted quotation marks.

Situation C

A winner would choose the tight-passive $10–$20 game. You can beat it even without catching cards. With a severely depleted bankroll, you must emphasize *survival.* You don't like the fact that you can't win much, but if you go broke, you can't win anything. So build up your bankroll *slowly.*

In fact, with such a small bankroll, many winners would look for an even smaller game. You should have 300 big bets, and you have only 100 big bets for this $10–$20 game.

The combination of a severe losing streak and a depleted bankroll can wipe out your confidence. Without confidence you can't play decisive, aggressive poker. So you need a win—even a small one—to build back your confidence.

All the other games are too risky, both financially and psychologically.

- You have only fifty big bets for the typical $20–$40, which is much too little.
- You have almost sixty-seven big bets for the wild $15–$30 game (which is still too little), but wild games have huge swings. If you get a run of bad cards, you're broke.
- You have the same number of big bets for the loose-passive $15–$30 game. It's tempting because loose-passive games are so easy to beat. Unfortunately, they also have fairly large swings, and you need the best hand to win. If you don't catch cards, you can go broke fairly quickly.

But what about your reputation? Everybody knows you're a $20–$40 player. If they see you playing $10–$20, they'll look down at you.

So what? Winners don't care that much about what people

think. They put the bottom line ahead of virtually everything. They know that—if they're on the rail—they can't win anything.

Situation D

Winners would ask friends for information about tomorrow's opponents. It's the best preparation they can do. However, because sleep is essential, they'd get to bed by 2 A.M.

They would not study any new book, not even *Harrington on Hold'em, Vol. II.* Trying to learn and apply new strategic concepts could easily confuse them.

Getting a good night's sleep is always a good idea, especially before a session that could be long, exhausting, and nerve-wracking. Unfortunately, you won't be able to sleep without taking sleeping pills, and they often cause a "hangover." You certainly can't afford one.

Drinking two glasses of wine just before playing would be a mistake. They may calm your nerves, but alcohol—even in limited quantities—reduces your brain's efficiency (even though many people don't believe it). You have to be sharp tomorrow.

Situation E

A winner would go home immediately. He would realize that thinking he can't do anything right probably means that he'll lose more money. He may be playing badly, or the opponents may be tougher than he thinks, or he may have a poor table image (or all three).

Deciding to keep playing until you lose your $100 stack is a mistake. First, that $100 is exactly as valuable as any other $100, but you probably don't value it that highly. You have passed what Mike Caro calls, "The Threshold of Pain." You believe (perhaps unconsciously), "I feel so bad now that I won't feel much worse if I lose another $100."

The real danger is not that you will lose that $100. It is that you will rebuy again and again and again.

But wait. Didn't you *promise* that you would quit if you lost that $100?

Of course you did, but such promises are often broken. Once you pass that Threshold of Pain, you may just keep going until you're broke. It's happened thousands of times.

Deciding to rebuy is even worse. If you lose all your cash and start going to the ATM, you will be *way* past your Threshold of Pain. You can easily lose your rent money (plus any money you can borrow).

Switching to the $2–$5 game is the worst choice. You're already off-balance. Since you know only two players, believing the game is pretty soft may be just wishful thinking. It's probably tougher than you believe, and you're not playing your best. Moving up because you are desperate to get even is one of the dumbest moves in poker.

Situation F

A winner would keep quiet and use the tell against his friend. Winners have a simple rule, "There are no friends at the poker table." They do whatever the rules and ethics allow to maximize their profits. Emphasizing profits is one of the biggest differences between winners and losers, and it affects almost everything they do.

A winner would not take it personally if a friend took advantage of his own tell or another weakness. Winners accept the game as it is, and they depersonalize conflicts.

Appendix B: Winners' Laws

This appendix will help you see the overall picture. It lists all these laws without any explanatory text. If you want some explanation, just go to the chapter. Please note that the introductory chapters to parts 2–6 and chapter 24 don't have any Winners' Laws.

Part One: Introduction

Chapter 1: Poker Winners Are *Really* Different
1. Learn how you compare to winners.
2. Commit yourself to making the necessary changes.

Chapter 2: Winners Are More Motivated and Disciplined
1. Accept a painful reality: intense, ruthless competitors have a *huge* edge.
2. Accept another painful reality: you can't make huge changes in your competitive drives and talent.
3. Assess your own talent and motivation honestly.
4. Work on your self-control.

Chapter 3: Winners Make Good Trade-Offs
1. Accept that trade-offs are unavoidable.
2. Accept that you can't satisfy all your motives.
3. Understand your own motives and priorities.
4. Learn which trade-offs each game or strategy requires.

5. Don't kid yourself.
6. Make the trade-offs that fit your priorities.

Chapter 4: Winners Manage Risks and Information Very Well

1. Do whatever it takes to get the best of it.
2. Get as much information as possible.
3. Give away as little information as possible.
4. When you get the best of it, act decisively to make the most of it.

Part Two: Winners Control Their Focus

Chapter 5: Winners Focus on Long-Term Results

1. Ask yourself constantly, Am I focusing on long-term results or short-term satisfactions?
2. Emphasize making good decisions, and minimize short-term results.
3. Record your wins and losses accurately.
4. Minimize everything else and focus on whatever improves your long-term results.

Chapter 6: Winners Focus on the Here and Now

1. Keep focused on what you should do *now* to maximize your long-term profits.
2. Accept that lost money, time, and effort are gone forever.
3. Pay attention to what you are thinking.

Chapter 7: Winners Focus on Power

1. Emphasize power, not luck, justice, or morality.
2. Constantly assess the power balance.
3. Constantly strive to become stronger.
4. Adjust your strategy to fit your power position.

Chapter 8: Winners Focus on Other People

1. Focus on other people, not yourself.
2. Apply the principle of "subjective rationality."
3. Objectively assess your opponents *every* time you play.
4. Relate to people on *their* terms.

Chapter 9: Winners Consider Complexities

1. Don't oversimplify.
2. Understand and work within your information-acquiring and information-processing limitations.
3. Select games that fit your strengths and weaknesses.

Part Three: Winners Control Their Thought Processes

Chapter 10: Winners Are Brutally Realistic

1. Admit that *you* overestimate some of your abilities and other virtues.
2. Admit that *you* have some unrealistic expectations.
3. Get objective assessments of yourself.
4. Select your games very carefully.

Chapter 11: Winners Think Logically

1. Accept that, unless you have great intuition, you *must* rely on logical thinking.
2. Don't assume that you have great intuition.
3. Develop your ability to think logically.

Chapter 12: Winners Prepare Thoroughly

1. Accept that preparation is absolutely essential.
2. Prepare systematically.

3. Use self-development "tools."
4. Use checklists.

Chapter 13: Winners Concentrate Intensely

1. Concentrate; give the game *all* your attention.
2. Select situations that minimize distractions.
3. Use "tools" to help you concentrate.
4. Don't feel obliged to "be polite."
5. Don't be too obvious.

Chapter 14: Winners Probe Efficiently

1. Probe frequently.
2. Use many probing methods.
3. Listen when other people probe.
4. Learn where and when to use various techniques.

Chapter 15: Winners Use Feedback Loops Well

1. Keep your mind open to new information.
2. Don't wait until your mistakes are obvious to everyone.
3. Keep accurate records.
4. Develop all the necessary skills.
5. Relate to people who will tell you the truth, *especially* when you don't want to hear it.
6. Make arrangements to get frequent, searching feedback.
7. Make it easy for others to provide helpful feedback.

Part Four: Winners Control the Information They Transmit

Chapter 16: Winners Are Judiciously Deceptive

1. Accept that deception is both legitimate and essential.

2. Analyze your own motives constantly.
3. Play deceptively or straightforward *only* when it increases your long-term profits.

Chapter 17: Winners Create the Right Images

1. Create the image that gives you the biggest edge in *this* situation, not the image that makes you most comfortable.
2. Make sure that your image is credible.
3. Base your image on a realistic assessment of yourself and your situation.
4. *Work* on your image.

Part Five: Winners Control Their Reactions to Feelings

Chapter 18: Winners Accept Poker As It Is

1. Accept that the "rules" are essentially fixed.
2. Accept that luck has enormous short-term effects, but trivial long-term ones.
3. Don't make excuses; accept responsibility for your results.

Chapter 19: Winners Depersonalize Conflicts

1. Keep your conflicts impersonal.
2. Know exactly where your interests conflict and coincide.
3. Use aggressive tactics *only* when they will improve your results, *never* just because you are upset.

Part Six: Winners Act Decisively

Chapter 20: Winners Are Selectively Aggressive

1. Accept that you *must* become selectively aggressive.

2. Compare your abilities and style to the competition and situation honestly.
3. Select the games you have the best chance of beating.
4. Select the best times and places to attack.

Chapter 21: Winners Push When They Are Winning
1. Push when you're winning.
2. Back off when you're losing.
3. Don't try too hard to "get even."
4. Look hard at your own motives.

Chapter 22: Winners Adjust Effectively to Changes
1. Accept that the only constant is change.
2. Ask frequently: "how is *my* game changing?"
3. Think frequently of how to adjust to these changes.
4. Develop the knowledge and skills you will need *before* you need them.
5. When you see that change is needed, *do it!*

Chapter 23: Winners Pay Their Dues
1. Accept that you *must* pay your dues.
2. Learn what the dues really are.
3. Learn how to pay them.
4. Make a plan for paying your dues.

Appendix C: How to Break Out of Your Comfort Zone

Everybody—even a top pro—has a comfort zone and dislikes going outside it. Because they are humans, not machines, even the biggest winners sometimes make emotionally based mistakes. However, because they are so motivated and disciplined, they do it far less often than you and I.

As I said in chapter 24, it is extremely difficult to break out of your comfort zone. To overcome the powerful forces that keep you from developing yourself, you should learn:

- What your comfort zone is
- How it affects your decisions
- How to break out of it

Definition

Your "comfort zone" is the situations and actions that seem natural and make you feel comfortable. The further you get from it, the more discomfort you will feel. It is quite individualistic because your likes and dislikes are different from other people's.

If we define "rational" as striving to maximize long-term profits, your desire to be comfortable is essentially irrational. You often pay a high long-term price to avoid short-term discomfort.

The term "comfort zone" is most often applied to the stakes, and many authorities recommend remaining in it because you will play better. If the stakes are too small, you will be bored and careless. If they are too high, you will be scared and indecisive.

You also have a comfort zone for many other issues, such as the number of players, their playing styles, tournaments versus cash games, a wide variety of specific plays, and your general playing style.

Your stylistic comfort zone affects virtually everything. For example, if you are very conservative, you will be more comfortable and get better results at ten-handed cash games. You can wait for good cards, which gives you an edge over loose players. If you play in shorthanded games or tournaments, you will have to break out of your comfort zone by playing more aggressively, or the blinds will eat you up.

The Comfort Zone Quandary

You may get the best short-term results by staying in your comfort zone, but—if you never venture outside it—you won't develop the qualities you need to:

- Increase your profits in your current game(s)
- Move up and make even bigger profits
- Adjust to changing circumstances

For example, if you never play for stakes above your comfort zone, you obviously can't develop the abilities you need to beat bigger games. If you never play in shorthanded games, you can't succeed in tournaments, nor can you exploit shorthanded games with weak players. If you don't experiment with uncomfortable moves, you'll often encounter situations that require plays you can't make.

The optimal balance between maximizing current profits and

developing yourself depends on your motives. If you are satisfied with your current results and are unwilling to sacrifice much to improve them, spend nearly all your time in your comfort zone. The more value you place on developing your game, the more often and the further you should break out of your comfort zone, but you must understand and accept the price: *You will probably reduce your short-term profits, and you will certainly become uncomfortable, perhaps extremely so.*

Resistance to Change

Millions of years of evolution and your own genes and experiences have programmed your body and mind to resist change. Your body has mechanisms to resist changes in temperature, blood pressure, chemical balances, and many other factors. In fact, your body codes most changes as "threats," and it automatically resists them.

Behavioral and psychological defenses are not as clearly defined and automatic, but they are extremely powerful. You, I, and everyone else have developed habits that help us to survive. We feel, "safe in our routines. . . . Our way is believed to be 'inherently right,' even when we know it is not."[1] Breaking these routines is extremely difficult because it feels so uncomfortable.

Poker writers generally assume (often without thinking about it) that people are rational, which we define as striving to maximize long-term profits. We tell people how to increase those profits and assume that they will follow our advice. But you and everyone else reduce long-term profits by making –EV plays. More importantly, thousands of psychological studies prove *why* everyone does it. *Short-term rewards and punishments—even trivial ones—have much greater impact than larger, but delayed, rewards and punishments.*

1. Dr. Daniel Kessler, personal e-mail to author, March 25, 2008.

For example, despite an enormous amount of information and social pressure, *most* American adults are overweight. The immediate pleasure and pain of eating and exercising have much greater effects than heart attacks, high blood pressure, diabetes, and obesity's other life-threatening, long-term effects. Millions of people smoke, including many doctors, despite knowing that they're killing themselves. Since people shorten their lives and damage their health for extremely small short-term pleasures, don't make the silly assumption that they're more rational about their poker chips.

Short-term rewards and punishments in poker are even more powerful than in most other activities because luck obscures the causal relationship between actions and long-term consequences.

> In most situations "people learn best through practice and feedback.... Unfortunately it does not work *at all* for poker. The immediate results in poker are often divorced from your actions.... You acted correctly, but your result was terrible.... Other times ... you acted incorrectly, but your result was terrific."[2]

The relationship between your actions and their long-term consequences is even more obscure in tough games. You can beat weak players just by playing technically correct poker. But in tough games, you must make deceptive plays to confuse your opponents. And "When you play deceptively, you are making a theoretical mistake (at least on this hand)."[3]

That is, you sacrifice some EV now by making a theoretical mis-

---

2. Ed Miller, David Sklansky, and Mason Malmuth, *Small Stakes Hold'em* (Henderson, NV: Two Plus Two, 2004), 17.

3. Barry Tanenbaum, "On Deception and Self-Deception: Part 1, *Poker Pages,* www.pokerpages.com/articles/archives/tanenbaum01.htm.

take, and you cannot be sure that the confusion you create will regain that lost EV. You may never know whether a "mistake" you made today caused an opponent to make a bigger mistake later in the session or even the next week.

Most other cause and effect relationships are much clearer. If you eat too much, you *know* that you will put on weight. You can even step on a scale and confirm it. Since you can't directly relate many poker actions to long-term consequences, the incentive to change is lessened, and the perceived value of breaking out of your comfort zone may be unclear.

Resistance to change also depends on the perceived risks of changing. The lower these risks are, the more willing you will be to take them. Reducing risk is an essential element of many forms of psychotherapy, especially group therapy. "The group setting may serve as a valuable way station, permitting patients to experiment with new behavior in a protected, low-risk environment."[4] You may dislike applying a group therapy concept to poker, but you will *certainly* be more willing to take small risks than large ones.

The risks of experimenting, the costs of making theoretical mistakes, the greater impact of short-term consequences, and the obscure cause and effect relationship are the primary reasons that so many people don't develop themselves.

Let's say that you are a solid, conservative, winning player, but your self-ratings indicate that you should play more aggressively and deceptively. You experiment by making a few raises and bluffs, which cost you some money. You were uncomfortable while making those plays and felt bad about losing the money.

Since you paid an immediate and clearly defined price in dis-

4. Irwin D. Yalom, *The Theory and Practice of Group Therapy* (NY: Basic Books, 1995), 406.

comfort and dollars, you may revert to your comfort zone. You feel bad *now,* while the future gains are almost abstractions. The pain of losing real dollars is much greater than the pleasure of winning the theoretical ones of long-term EV. Perhaps the most difficult problem in breaking out of your comfort zone is *to shift your focus from short-term to long-term rewards and punishments.*

Resistance to Changing Your Style

This resistance is extremely powerful. Your style affects virtually everything, and it was caused by the same factors that created your basic personality. "People play the style of game they are comfortable playing. Aggressive people play aggressively, and passive people play passively.... Players fall into a comfort zone."[5]

If you want to become a bigger winner, you must understand what your style is, where it fits, and when and how to change it. As Barry Tanenbaum put it, "This book will ask you to make plays outside your current comfort zone.... You must be prepared to tolerate (if not embrace) these new and uncomfortable circumstances to make more money at poker."[6]

I wholeheartedly agree, but just wanting to break out of your comfort zone does not mean that you will do it. If you doubt me, just look at your other self-improvement attempts. How many times have you tried and failed to lose weight, stop smoking, or exercise regularly? Since you gain immeasurably more from them than from improving your poker, don't expect to make large

5. Barry Tanenbaum, *Advanced Limit Hold'em Strategy* (West Sussex, UK: D & B Publishing, 2007), 44.

6. Tanenbaum, Advanced Limit Hold'em, 44–47.

changes in your poker-playing style without a great deal of work and discomfort.

Because there is no databased research on how to change your poker style, I have borrowed from the hundreds of investigations of dieting and exercising programs. This research provides *overwhelming* evidence that hardly anyone who starts a program makes large, long-term changes in their weight or physical condition.

Some people never really get started. Others make significant improvements for a short time, but soon revert to their old habits. The fault is usually *not* with the program. It would work, but people don't stick to it.

Some people believe that this research is irrelevant because "poker is different." They have absolutely no evidence to support their position, while there is enormous evidence that an extremely wide variety of self-improvement plans fail. Since people don't stick to programs to reduce their weight, get in shape, quit smoking, learn Spanish, get a degree, and so on, it is absurd to claim that different principles apply to poker.

In addition, the same factors that cause people to play in certain ways cause them to act that way in other situations. Aggressive gamblers are likely to be impatient, make risky investments, choose jobs that reward performance rather than seniority, dislike rigid routines, drive aggressively, and so on. Deceptive players enjoy keeping others off-balance. Conservative players tend to be patient, drive carefully, save their money, and buy lots of insurance.

A few very disciplined people play poker differently from the way they act in other situations. If you are one of those people, making the recommended changes will be fairly easy. The more your poker style expresses your basic personality, the harder it will be to change it.

I have borrowed concepts from four poker authors. They do *not* have any scientifically acceptable data, but they have thought carefully about the problems and processes of changing styles.

- Mike Caro has often written about "Missions."[7] A Mission is *one* change you want to make. He recommends playing in your usual way, while making *only* that change. His mission concept is the foundation of chapter 24's step-by-step program.
- Barry Tanenbaum wrote about "Overcoming Obstacles,"[8] and we have often discussed his use of Caro-type missions to expand his students' comfort zones. For example, he may tell a passive student to become more aggressive preflop by never open-limping.
- David Sklansky discussed the problems of changing yourself with me and referred me to his article "Will Power."[9] It directly relates improving poker to the same kinds of willpower needed to stick to dieting, exercising, and other self-improvement programs.
- David Apostolico wrote "Changing from the Outside In." His basic principle was "act in a certain way and you will feel in a certain way," but do it when your chances of success are high. Then "take the action and see where it takes you."[10]

7. Mike Caro used the term in *Twelve Days to Hold'em Success* and *Caro's Most Profitable Hold'em Advice*.

8. Tanenbaum, *Advanced Limit Hold'em Strategy*, 44–50.

9. David Sklansky, "Will Power," in *Fighting Fuzzy Thinking in Poker, Gaming, and Life* (Henderson, NV: Two Plus Two, 1997), 21–22.

10. David Apostolico, "Changing from the Outside In," *Card Player*, January 2, 2008.

To increase your chances of taking all eleven steps listed in chapter 24, ask yourself:

- What is my style?
- What does it cost me to play that way?
- Why do I play that way?

What Is My Style?

Carefully examine all the self-ratings, looking for a pattern among them. You will probably see that you need to become:

- Tighter
- Or more aggressive
- Or more deceptive
- Or all three

You may also see that you need to become less emotional, talkative, and so on. For the moment, let's stay focused on tightness, aggression, and deceptiveness.

What Does It Cost Me to Play That Way?

To increase your motivation to change, try to determine your style's *specific* costs. For example, you may find that you don't get enough action on your big hands because you aren't deceptive enough. Or you may learn that you win a relatively small percentage of the pots you contest until showdown because you're too loose.

Why Do I Play That Way?

You have probably chosen the style that is natural and comfortable. So the obvious question is: *Why* do you feel that way?

You may not know because nearly everyone misunderstands and oversimplifies their motives. Virtually everything you do is driven by multiple motives and thought processes, and they often conflict with each other. Your genes and a lifetime of experiences have made you what you are today, and your desire to think well of yourself reduces your objectivity. If you get feedback from a coach, poker buddy, online forum, or discussion group, you will get a more accurate picture.

Don't look only at your poker playing. Look for similarities between poker and your actions in many other places. For example,

- Are your home and desk neat or messy?
- Do you interrupt other people, or let them interrupt you?
- Are you patient or impatient in slow-moving lines?
- Are you so uncomfortable when you lie or bluff that other people can see right through you?

These types of questions will help you understand how your personality affects your poker playing. The more deeply imbedded your poker style is in your overall personality, the harder it will be to change it.

Let's get personal. Because my friends are honest with me, I have reluctantly accepted that I am too conservative. It costs me both chips and respect, but that style fits my personality. Many people of my age and background have the same conservative approach, not just to poker, but to almost everything. We save money, drive carefully, invest cautiously, avoid arguments, own lots of insurance, and so on.

By working hard, I have changed very, very slowly. I'm still not aggressive enough, but I'm a lot better than I once was. The same principle applies to you. To make fundamental changes in the way you play, you must work hard and accept that your progress will be slow. But—if you really want to develop yourself—it's worth the time and effort.

Index

Abilities. *See also* Skills
   overestimating your, 102–5, 108
Acceptance (accepting poker as it is),
      204–12
   author's personal confession,
      209–10
   bad beat stories, 205–6
   learning how to lose, 206
   of people as they are, 209
   rating yourself, 211
   of responsibility for results, 208,
      211
   of the rules, 207–8, 210–11
   of selective aggression, 231–32
   vicious and virtuous cycles, 209
   Winners' Laws, 210–11
Ace on the River (Greenstein), 16
Achievable goals, 272
Acting decisively. *See* Decisive action
Adjustments (adjusting to changes),
      241–48
   continuing professional education,
      245–46
   long-term changes, 243–45
   rating yourself, 247
   short-term changes, 242–43
   Winners' Laws, 246–47
   to your opponents, 92–93
Advanced Limit Hold'em Strategy
      (Tanenbaum), 126, 145n, 221n
Affection vs. profits, 34
Aggressive play, 123–24, 179. *See also*
      Selective aggression
America's Cup, 207n
Angelo, Tommy, 103, 122, 128–29,
      136–37, 148, 171, 209–10, 251
Anger (angry players), 149, 202
Apostolico, David, 76, 297
Art of War (Sun Tzu), 120

Asking questions, 143–45, 147,
      148–49
Asmo, Louis, 149, 171–72
Auerbach, Arnold Jacob "Red," 14

Bad beat stories, 169–72, 205–6
Bad luck. *See* Luck
Balance, and self-control, 16–18
Bankroll
   paying your dues, 253–54
   rewards vs. risks, 29–30
   Sklansky on, vii–viii
   as source of power, 78–79
Bets (betting), as probing technique,
      141–42, 143
Biases, 159–61. *See also* Rating
      yourself
Bird, Larry, 14
Bluffs (bluffing), 182–83
Body language. *See* Tells
Book of Bluffs (Lessinger), 182–83
Book of Tells (Caro), 131, 136, 144
Brunson, Doyle, 84, 112, 114, 136, 157,
      206, 215, 237–38
Brutal realism, 101–10, 203
   about the game, 107
   about opponents, 106
   about yourself, 102–5, 108
   feedback loops and, 154–55
   rating yourself, 109
   Winners' Laws, 107–9
Buddies, 108, 267–68
Bully image, 189

Calls (calling), as probing technique,
      141–42, 143
Card Player, 105, 118–19, 136, 244,
      246
Caro, Mike, 85n, 131, 136, 144, 297

Changes
adjusting to. *See* Adjustments
resistance to, 271–72, 292–98
Checklists, 133
Checks (checking), as probing
technique, 141–42, 143
Chess-type thinking, 125–26
Chiu, David, 149, 171–72
Ciaffone, Bob, 153
Cincinnati Kid, The (movie), 229
Closed-ended questions, 144–45,
148–49
Coaches (coaching), 108, 164, 267–68
Coin flips, 71–72
Comfort zone, 290–300
defined, 290–91
resistance to change and, 292–98
Comfort zone quandary, 291–92
Comments (commenting), 62–63,
145–46, 192–93
Competitiveness (competitive drive),
14–15, 19
Complaints (complaining publicly),
170, 205–6, 207
Complexities, 90–95
adjusting to your opponents, 92–93
information overload, 94
"it depends on the situation,"
90–92
mental speed and, 93–94
rating yourself, 95
Winners' Laws, 94–95
Compliments, 145–46
Computer simulations, 118–19, 133,
244–45
Concentration, 135–40
rating yourself, 139
Winners' Laws, 138–39
Conflict personalization, 213–17
Connors, Barbara, 169
Continuing professional education,
245–46
Control
of focus. *See* Focus
of information. *See* Information
management
of reaction to feelings. *See*
Reactions to feelings
of thought processes. *See* Thought
processes

Cooke, Roy, 59n, 101, 105, 136, 186,
199, 249
Crazy gambles, 190–91
Credible image, 191, 194

Dalla, Nolan, 10, 103n, 117, 122
Dandolos, Nick "The Greek," 10, 57–58
Darwin, Charles, 243–44
Dead money, 58, 229–30
Deception (deceptiveness), 172,
174–85
bluffing, 182–83
how should you be, 178–82
rating yourself, 184
vs. profits, 35
when should you be, 175–78
Winners' Laws, 183–84
Decisive action, 17–18, 50–51,
221–56
adjusting effectively to changes,
241–48
paying your dues, 249–56
pushing when winning, 234–40
selective aggression, 225–33
Delusions, 102, 159–61. *See also*
Brutal realism
Depersonalizing conflicts, 213–17
rating yourself, 217
Winners' Laws, 216
Destructive emotions, 200, 202
Development, 63–64
of skills, 132, 163, 246–47, 252
profits vs., 33–34
training tools, 118–19
Diet, 119–20
Discipline, 13–23, 203
need for balance, 16–18
rating yourself, 21–23
ruthless need to win, 14–15, 18
as source of power, 78
Winners' Laws, 18–21
Discussion groups, 108, 120
Distractions, 137–38
Dolan, Phil, 213
Doyle Brunson's Super System
(Brunson), 112, 237–38
Dues, 249–56
costs of not paying, 253–54
rating yourself, 256
skills hierarchy, 253

what you must pay, 251–52
Winners' Laws, 255
Dynamic thinking, 158–59

Edge, 75. *See also* Power
Education of a Poker Player (Yardley), 244
Efficient probing, 141–52
  during and after the hand, 142
  downsides of, 149–50
  rating yourself, 151
  techniques for, 142–48
  timing your, 148–49
  Winners' Laws, 150–51
Ego (egotism), 61–62, 99
  vs. profits, 35–36
Elements of Poker (Angelo), 128–29
Emotions (emotional reactions), 199–217
  accepting poker as it is, 204–12
  depersonalizing conflicts, 213–17
  destructive, 200, 202
  general effects of, 201
  television effects on, 202–3
  winners control of, 203
Entitlement mentality, 250–51, 254
Exercise, 119–20
Expected value (EV), 43–46, 71–72
  calculating, 44–45
  long-term results and, 60–62
  poker and, 45–46
  Sklansky on, vii–viii
Exploitation vs. profits, 35
Extreme discipline, 16. *See also* Discipline

Fairness vs. power, 76–77, 81
Fame vs. profits, 31–32
Fancy Play Syndrome, 178
Fear, uncertainty, and doubt (FUD), 188–89
Feedback loops, 153–65, 241
  assessing opponents' strengths, weaknesses, and styles, 158–59
  assessing yourself, 159–62
  characteristics of, 155, 157–58
  rating yourself, 165
  reading opponents cards, 156–58
  Winners' Laws, 163–64
Feeney, John, 61*n*, 67

First impressions, 158–59
Fish, 229–30
Fixed-limit poker, and deception, 177–78
Flack, Layne, 114, 136
Flynn, Matt, 126*n*
Focus, 55–95
  on complexities, 90–95
  on the here and now, 67–74, 235–36
  on long-term results, 57–66
  on other people, 84–89
  on power, 75–83
Folding, reviewing play after, 127–28
Forgiveness (forgiving yourself), 274–75
Free lunches, 24
Friedman, Milton, 24, 36
Fromm, David, 11*n*, 93*n*, 158–59, 187–88, 190–91
Frustration avoidance vs. profits, 28–29
Fundamental Theorem of Poker, 47–48, 169
Fun vs. profits, 28
Future (future sessions), preparing for, 72, 129–32

Game rejection, 122
Game selection, 95, 109, 121–22, 210, 228–30, 232
Gentle criticisms, 146
Gentle probes, 145
Giving away information, 169–72, 201, 205–6
Goals, setting achievable, 272
Good health, 119–20
Greenstein, Barry, 16, 33, 229
Gregorich, Mark, 249
Grudzien, Nick, 244*n*

Hackworth, David, 117
Hamlet, 17–18
Handicap, 207
Hands
  preparing to play, 124–28
  probing during and after, 142
Hand-tracking software, 118–19, 133, 244–45
Harrington, Dan, 86*n*
Harrison, Lizzy, 229*n*

Hellmuth, Phil, 105
Herzog, Geoff, 244n
Hesitating, and probing, 147–48
Hit and run (hitting and running),
    236–37
Homework. *See* Preparation
How Do You Rate. *See* Rating
    yourself
*How To Dominate $1 and $2 No Limit
    Hold'em* (O'Connor), 221

"I'm a bully" image, 189
Image, 172–73, 186–95
    general principles, 191–92
    losers' mistakes, 192–94
    preparing to play each hand and,
        124–25
    rating yourself, 195
    types of, 187–91
    Winners' Laws, 194–95
"I'm a loser" image, 187–89
"I'm a sucker" image, 190
"I'm a wild gambler" image, 190–91
"I'm a winner" image, 187–89
Impatience, 214, 231
Impersonal conflicts, 214–16
Impulsiveness, 214
Indecisive players, 17–18, 50–51
Information management, 42–43,
        46–52, 169–95
    central principles of, 46–48
    creating right images, 186–95
    decisive players and, 50–51
    interdependence of risk and, 43,
        46–47
    judicious deceptiveness, 174–85
    rating yourself, 52
    role of luck, 51
    Winners' Laws, 51–52
Information overload, 94
Intermediate-term information, about
        opponents, 87
Intuition (intuitive approach), 111–16,
        136, 157
    defined, 111–12
    rating yourself, 116
    Winners' Laws, 115–16
IQ, average, 19–20
"It depends on the situation," 90–92

Jacoby, Oswald, 63, 244
Johnson, Linda, 104, 121
Jones, Lee, 177
Judicious deceptiveness. *See*
    Deception
Justice vs. power, 76–77, 81

Kessler, Daniel, 267–68, 292n
Knowledge of play, 118–19, 246–47
Krieger, Lou, 204, 249

Leitner, Jim, 142n
Lessinger, Matt, 33–34, 90, 182–83,
        241
Logic (logical thinking), 111–16,
        136
    defined, 111–12
    rating yourself, 116
    Winners' Laws, 115–16
Long-term changes, and making
        adjustments, 243–45
Long-term information, about
        opponents, 86
Long-term results (profits), 57–66
    dangers of focusing on anything
        but, 58–59
    expected value and, 60–62
    losers' beliefs and, 61–62
    rating yourself, 66
    short-term results vs., 59–60, 63–64,
        65
    short-term satisfactions vs., 62–63,
        64–65
    Winners' Laws, 64–65
Loose-aggressive players, and
        deception, 179
Loose-passive players, and deception,
        179–80
Loser image, 187–89
Losers vs. winners
    role of skill and talent, 9–11
    sample situations, 4–8
        textbook answers, 279–83
    what you learned about yourself,
        8–9
Losing streaks, 206, 234–35
Lovinger, Jay, 3
Luck, 51, 107, 211, 234–35
    vs. power, 76–77, 81

Machiavelli, Niccolò, 76
Machiavellian Poker Strategy
(Apostolico), 76
McQueen, Steve, 229
Magic formula trap, 92
Malmuth, Mason, 42, 44n, 45n, 51,
62n, 79n, 85n, 92n, 111, 113,
124, 136, 208n, 228, 254, 293n
Maniacs, 226, 242–43
Mehta, Sunny, 126n
Mental speed, 93–94, 124–25
Mentors, 267–68
Miller, Ed, 45n, 62n, 113, 126n,
177–78, 208n, 293n
Miranda Warning, 129
Misa, Jason, 13
Morality vs. power, 76–77, 81
Moss, Johnny, 9–10, 57, 118, 119, 135
Motives (motivation), 13–23
brutal realism about, 102–5
deceptiveness and, 178, 184
extreme discipline, 16
feedback loops and, 162
focus and, 55–56
need for balance, 16–18
of opponents, 86
for playing poker, 25–27, 36, 37
rating yourself, 21–22
ruthless need to win, 14–15, 18
Winners' Laws, 18–21
Mum Poker, 171

Navarro, Joe, 131, 136, 144
Negotiate to Win (Schoonmaker),
153n
Negreanu, Dan, 104, 206
Newton, Isaac, 119
Nguyen, Scotty, 206–7
No-limit poker, and deception,
177–78
Notes. *See* Records

Oade, Preston, 32, 199n
O'Connor, Sam, 221
Olney, Don, 249
Olympians, 10–11, 119
Open-ended questions, 144–45,
148–49
Open mind, to new information, 163

Opponents
accepting as they are, 209
adjusting to, 92–93
deceptiveness and, 176–82
feedback loops and, 155–59
focusing on, 84–89
intermediate-term information
about, 87
long-term information about, 86
preparing at the table before
playing, 123–24
preparing for future hands, 127–29
preparing for future sessions,
129–32
realism about, 106
short-term information about,
84–86
Winners' Laws, 87–88
Oswald Jacoby on Poker (Jacoby), 244
Othmer, Konstantin, 190n, 228n
Overestimation, 102–5, 108
Oversimplification, 91–92, 94

Passive-aggressive play, 123–24
Pauses (pausing), after probing, 147
Paying your dues. *See* Dues
Personal abilities. *See* Abilities; Skills
Personal development, 63–64
of skills, 132, 163, 246–47, 252
profits vs., 33–34
training tools, 118–19
Personalizing conflicts, 213–17
Personal motives. *See* Motives
Physical health, 119–20
Poker books, 243–44, 249–50
Poker buddies, 108, 267–68
Poker face, 171
Poker fantasies, and realism about
yourself, 102–5
Politeness, 139
Political correctness, 106
Position, 124–25, 242
attacking when in good, 227–28
as source of power, 79–81, 82
Pot-limit poker, and deception, 177–78
Pot size, and deception, 177
Power, 75–83
bankroll as source of, 78–79
frequent changes in, 80–81

Power *(cont.)*
    Machiavelli on, 76–77
    position as source of, 79–81, 82
    rating yourself, 82
    as relative, 77
    skill and discipline as source of, 78
    Winners' Laws, 81–82
Prejudice, 106
Preparation, 117–34
    developing knowledge and skills,
        118–19
    for future hands, 127–29
    for future sessions, 129–32
    to play each hand, 124–27
    rating yourself, 134
    selecting best game, 121–22
    selecting best seat, 122–23
    for specific events, 120–21
    staying healthy, 119–20
    at table before playing, 123–24
    Winners' Laws, 132–33
Prince, The (Machiavelli), 76
Probing, 141–52
    during and after the hand, 142
    downsides of, 149–50
    rating yourself, 151
    techniques for, 142–48
    timing your, 148–49
    Winners' Laws, 150–51
Professional education, 245–46
Professional No-limit Hold'em (Flynn,
        Mehta and Miller), 126
Profits. *See also* Long-term results
    vs. affection, 34
    vs. avoiding frustration, 28–29
    vs. being deceptive and
        exploitative, 35
    vs. developing your skills, 33–34
    vs. ego building, 35–36
    vs. fun, 28
    vs. status and fame, 31–32
    vs. testing yourself against tough
        competition, 33
    vs. variance, 30–31
Promiscuously aggressive play, 226
Psychological edge, 75. *See also*
        Power
Psychology of Poker (Schoonmaker),
        25*n*, 31, 114, 123, 124, 131,
        146, 178–82, 193*n*, 205, 227*n*

Pushing, 234–40
    rating yourself, 239
    self-fulfilling prophecies, 236–38
    Winners' Laws, 238–39

Questions, asking, 143–45, 147,
        148–49
Quitting (quit decision), 70–71

Raise (raising), as probing technique,
        141–42, 143
Rating yourself, 257–75
    steps to take to change yourself,
        267–75
Rationalizations, 64*n*, 252, 292
Reactions to feelings, 199–217
    accepting poker as it is, 204–12
    depersonalizing conflicts, 213–17
    general effects of, 201
    television effects on, 202–3
    winners control of, 203
Read 'em and Reap (Navarro), 131,
        136, 144
Reading, 85–86, 156–58
Realism, 101–10, 203
    about the game, 107
    about opponents, 106
    about yourself, 102–5, 108
    feedback loops and, 154–55
    rating yourself, 109
    Winners' Laws, 107–9
Reber, Arthur, 204
Records (record keeping), 65, 160–61,
        163, 228–29, 272–73
Relative, power as, 77
Reliability, and feedback loops, 155,
        157–58
Resistance to change, 271–72, 292–98
Rewards vs. risks, 29–30
Right image. *See* Image
Ringer, Robert, 189
Risk avoiders, 42–43
Risk management, 42–52
    central principle of, 43–45
    expected value and, 45–46
    interdependence of information
        and, 43, 46–47
    rating yourself, 52
    Winners' Laws, 51–52
Risk reduction, 294

Risk/reward ratio (RRR), 182
Risk seekers, 43
Risks vs. rewards, as trade-off, 29–30
Robertie, Bill, 86n
Roberts, Brian "Sailor," 119
Robinson, Edward G., 229
Rocks, 242–43
Rules, acceptance of, 207–8, 210–11
Rushes, 237–38
Ruthlessness, 14–15, 18

Scared play, 78
Scarne, John, 225
Seat selection, 122–23
Selective aggression, 225–33
  attacking weaker players, 230–31
  attacking when in good position,
      227–28
  game selection and, 228–30
  rating yourself, 233
  waiting for right cards, 226–27
  Winners' Laws, 231–32
Self-assessment, 159–62. See also
      Rating yourself
Self-control, 13–23, 203. See also
      Focus
  extreme discipline, 16
  need for balance, 16–18
  rating yourself, 21–23
  ruthless need to win, 14–15, 18
  as source of power, 78
  Winners' Laws, 18–21
Self-fulfilling prophecies, 236–38
Self-pity, 162, 170, 202, 208
Self-ratings. See Rating yourself
Sensitivity, and feedback loops, 155,
      157–58
Sexton, Mike, 208n
Short-term changes, and making
      adjustments, 242–43
Short-term information, about
      opponents, 84–86
Short-term results, dangers of
      focusing on, 59–60, 63–64, 65,
      270–71, 292–94
Short-term satisfactions, 62–63,
      64–65
Showing your cards, 171–72
Shulman, Barry, 75, 160n
Simplification, 91–92, 94

Single-mindedness, 14–15, 18, 49. See
      also Focus
Skills
  developing your, 132, 163, 246–47,
      252
    profits vs., 33–34
    training tools, 118–19
  hierarchy of, 253
  as source of power, 78
  winners vs. losers, 9–11
Sklansky, David, vii–viii, 45n, 47n, 48,
      51, 57–58, 61n, 62n, 70n, 79n,
      85, 91–92, 113, 125–26, 132,
      136, 156–57, 169, 174, 175–78,
      208n, 234, 270, 293n, 297
Sleep, 119–20
Socrates, 40
Specific events, preparing for, 120–21
Speed, and feedback loops, 155,
      157–58
Stakes, and deceptiveness, 176–77
Status vs. profits, 31–32
Stay-or-quit rules, 70–71
Stratified games, 10–11
Straus, Jack, 14–15, 119
Studying. See Preparation
Stylistic comfort zone. See Comfort
      zone
Subjective rationality, 87–88
Sucker image, 190
Sun Tzu, 120
Supercompetitors, 16–18
Super System (Brunson), 112, 237–38
Swapping mistakes, 177–78

Table image. See Image
Talent, 9–11, 19–22
Tanenbaum, Barry, 64, 67, 126,
      129–30, 131, 141, 143, 145,
      175–76, 178n, 188–89, 221,
      249, 253, 274–75, 293n, 295,
      297
Television, 32, 202–3
Tells, 85–86, 131, 136, 144, 171
Theorem of Poker, 47–48, 169
Theory of Poker (Sklansky), 91–92,
      175–76
Thought processes, 99–165
  brutal realism, 101–10
  concentration, 135–40

Thought processes *(cont.)*
  feedback loops, 153–65
  logical thinking, 111–16
  preparing thoroughly, 117–34
  probing efficiently, 141–52
Tight-aggressive players, 226–27. *See also* Selective aggression
  deception and, 180–82
Tight-loose players, 123–24
Tight-passive players, and deception, 180
Tilt, 206, 234–35
Time pressures, 124–25
Trade-offs, 24–41
  motives for playing poker, 24–27
  personal definition of "winning," 39–41
  rating yourself, 38–39
  Winners' Laws, 36–38
Training tools, 118–19, 133, 244–45

Ungar, Stu, 9–10, 114, 238
Unpredictability, and deceptiveness, 174, 176

Variance vs. profits, 30–31
Vicious cycles, 209
Victim image, 208
Virtuous cycles, 209
Vulnerability, 201, 202, 214

Waiting for right cards, 226–27
War games, 120
Weak players, 75, 154, 230–31
"What if" contingency planning, 91–92
Whining, 204, 205–6, 208, 254
Wild Gambler image, 190–91
Winner image, 187–89
Winners' Laws, 11–12, 284–89
  acceptance, 210–11
  adjusting to changes, 246–47
  brutal realism, 107–9
  complexities, 94–95

concentration, 138–39
deceptiveness, 183–84
depersonalizing conflicts, 216
efficient probing, 150–51
feedback loops, 163–64
here and now, 73
logical thinking, 115–16
long-term results, 64–65
motivation and discipline, 18–21
opponents, focus on, 87–88
paying your dues, 255
power, 81–82
preparation, 132–33
pushing when winning, 238–39
right image, 194–95
risk and information management, 51–52
selective aggression, 231–32
trade-offs, 36–38
Winners vs. losers
  role of skill and talent, 9–11
  sample situations, 4–8
    textbook answers, 279–83
  what you learned about yourself, 8–9
Winning Low Limit Hold'em (Jones), 177
"Winning," personal definition of, 39–41
Winning Through Intimidation (Ringer), 189
Woods, Tiger, 164
"Woulda, coulda, shoulda" games, 72

Yalom, Irwin D., 294n
Your Best Poker Friend (Schoonmaker), 15n, 63n, 162, 164n, 238n
Your Worst Poker Enemy (Schoonmaker), 129n, 200n, 202, 203, 243n, 245n

Zee, Ray, 11n, 93n, 113, 122–23, 158–59, 187–88, 190–91

About the Author

Alan Schoonmaker has a unique combination of academic credentials, business experience, and poker expertise. After earning a Ph.D. in industrial psychology from The University of California at Berkeley, he joined the faculties at UCLA and Carnegie-Mellon University. He then became a research fellow at Belgium's Catholic University of Louvain.

He was the manager of management development at Merrill Lynch before starting Schoonmaker and Associates, an international consulting company. He personally taught or consulted in twenty-nine countries on all six continents for clients such as GE, GM, IBM, Mobil, Rank Xerox, Bankers Trust, Wells Fargo, Manufacturers Hanover, Chemical Bank, Chase Manhattan, Ryan Homes, Sun Life of Canada, and more than two dozen others. His personal clients' annual sales greatly exceed one trillion dollars.

Schoonmaker has written or co-authored three research monographs and has published four books on industrial psychology *(Anxiety and the Executive, Executive Career Strategy, Selling: The Psychological Approach,* and *Negotiate to Win),* one book on coping with college *(A Student's Survival Manual),* and three books on poker *The Psychology of Poker. Your Worst Poker Enemy* and *Your Best Poker Friend.* His books have been translated into French, German, Spanish, Swedish, Portuguese, Japanese, and Indonesian.

Over one hundred articles in poker and business periodicals such as *Card Player, Poker Digest,* twoplustwo.com's *Internet Magazine,* Andy Glazer's *Wednesday Night Poker, The California Man-*

agement Review, and *Expansion* have been published. He has written or played (or both) the leading role in four video series. Two were parts of multimedia training programs on industrial psychology. At one time his *Selling: The Psychological Approach* was the world's best-selling computer-based program for business people.

He has served as an expert witness about poker psychology in both an administrative hearing and a lawsuit. He played online poker as a member of RoyalVegasPoker.com's team of experts. He has been interviewed several times on radio and television about both poker and industrial psychology. He has also hosted about forty radio shows on Holdemradio.com and roundersradio.com.

Many requests are received for coaching, but most of these requests are referred to friends because he is not an expert on poker strategy. He accepts a small number of clients who need coaching *only* on poker psychological issues such as controlling impulses, coping with losing streaks, going on tilt, and planning your poker career.

He welcomes readers' questions and comments at alannschoonmaker@hotmail.com and alan_schoonmaker@yahoo.com.